DOES GOD

CARE HOW WE

WORSHIP?

DOES GOD

CARE HOW WE

WORSHIP?

LIGON DUNCAN

P U B L I S H I N G
P.O. BOX 817 • PHILLIPSBURG • NEW JERSEY 08865-0817

Did you find this book helpful?
Consider leaving a review online.
The author appreciates your feedback!

Or write to P&R at editorial@prpbooks.com
with your comments. We'd love to hear from you.

The material presented here was originally published in *Give Praise to God: A Vision for Reforming Worship: Celebrating the Legacy of James Montgomery Boice*, edited by Philip Graham Ryken, Derek W. H. Thomas, and J. Ligon Duncan III (Phillipsburg, NJ: P&R Publishing, 2003), pp. 17–73. Content has been edited for this new format.

Printed in the United States of America

Names: Duncan, J. Ligon, 1960- author.
Title: Does God care how we worship? / Ligon Duncan.
Description: Phillipsburg, New Jersey : P&R Publishing, 2020. | "Originally published in Give Praise to God: A Vision for Reforming Worship: Celebrating the Legacy of James Montgomery Boice, edited by Philip Graham Ryken, Derek W. H. Thomas, and J. Ligon Duncan III (Phillipsburg, NJ: P&R Publishing, 2003), pp. 17-73. Content has been edited for this new format." | Summary: "The Reformed church is notable for its biblically regulated worship. Ligon Duncan describes the principles God gives us for worship and how we can put them in action today"-- Provided by publisher.
Identifiers: LCCN 2019046813 | ISBN 9781629957920 (paperback)
Subjects: LCSH: Public worship--Reformed Church. | Reformed Church--Doctrines.
Classification: LCC BX9427 .D86 2020 | DDC 264/.042--dc23
LC record available at https://lccn.loc.gov/2019046813

CONTENTS

FOREWORD

Over twenty years ago now, I was asked to speak to a gathering of pastors (largely Presbyterian) on worship. The setting was the Presbyterian Church in America's Convocation on Reformation and Revival. It took place in a decade marked by gathering strength for what would come to be known as the "young, restless, and Reformed" movement. In September of 1999, I had the privilege not only of speaking on this topic but of hearing others as well.

There was no clearer teaching at that convocation than that given by my friend Ligon Duncan, a professor of theology at the Reformed Theological Seminary. Over twenty years later, I still regularly refer to my notes from Ligon's wise teaching. Here are just some of the jewels Ligon shared with us in those days.

- The regulative principle frees us from bondage to the whims of men.
- The doctrine of worship is a subset of the doctrine of the church.
- There is a god we want and a God who is, and the two are not the same.

- The basic problem of humanity is not atheism, it is idolatry.
- Adding to God's Word is like taking away from it.

The pages that follow will further clarify and explain these points. I urged him to publish. Just a few years later, Ligon and Phil Ryken published a festschrift for the late James Montgomery Boice. Its first two chapters were Ligon's teaching that I had so treasured—cleaned up, more fully and systematically organized, but with all the jewels of wisdom and prudence that had first struck me. In these pages, we find the historic Reformed understanding of the Bible's teaching on how we approach God, freshly considered and laid out in a clear, introductory fashion.

When too many Christians today are wandering around in the darkness of self-imposed ignorance, how brilliant a discovery it is that God's Word sheds plenty of light on our regular times together in corporate worship. Read and profit.

Mark Dever
Senior Pastor, Capitol Hill Baptist Church
Washington, DC

PART ONE

DOES GOD CARE HOW
WE WORSHIP?

THE BIBLE AS THE KEY TO REFORMING WORSHIP

If a renewal of Christian worship is to be undertaken, on what principle will it be founded? If we are to live and worship together *soli deo gloria*, then what shall be the basis and pattern? The only answer for the evangelical Christian is *sola scriptura*. God's Word itself must supply the principles and patterns and content of Christian worship. True Christian worship is by the book. It is according to Scripture. The Bible alone ultimately directs the form and content of Christian worship.

This is a Reformational emphasis, which came to fruition especially in the Reformed branch of the great Protestant Reformation of the sixteenth century (in contrast to the Lutheran and Radical Reformation traditions and in direct contradiction of the Roman Catholic tradition). It is found in Calvin and other first-generation Reformed theologians. It is found in John Knox and the Scottish tradition. It is found in the Puritan tradition of the Church of England, from the days of Elizabeth I to the Commonwealth and thereafter in English Nonconformity. It is firmly established in the Baptist confessions and in the Congregational creeds.

This strong and special emphasis on the corporate worship of God being founded positively on the directions of Scripture came to be known as the regulative principle. It is an extension of the Reformational axiom of *sola scriptura*. As the Bible is the final authority in faith and life, so it is also the final authority in how we corporately worship—but in a distinct and special way. Whereas all of life is to be lived in accordance with Scripture, Scripture does not speak discreetly to every specific component of our lives. There are many situations in which we must rely upon general biblical principles and then attempt to think Christianly without specific guidance in various circumstances.

The Reformers thought the matter of corporate worship was just a little bit different from this. They taught that God had given full attention to this matter in his word because it is one of central significance in the Christian life and in his eternal purposes. Therefore, we are to exercise a special kind of care when it comes to this activity—a care distinct from that which we employ anywhere else in the Christian life. He told us what to do and how to do it, in such a way that the prime aspects of worship are a matter of following divine direction; and thus the decisions that remain to be made by us—thinking in accordance with the general principles of Scripture and sanctified common sense, in the absence of positive scriptural warrant—are relatively minor. It is not difficult to find this axiom being articulated, in various ways, from the earliest days of the Reformed tradition to our own time—and in all the representative branches of the Reformed community.

For instance, Calvin said: "God disapproves of all modes of worship not expressly sanctioned by His Word."[1] The Continental Reformed tradition, reflected in the Belgic Confession (article 32) and the Heidelberg Catechism (Q. 96), asserts the same. The Second London Baptist Confession of 1689 and the Philadelphia (Baptist) Confession of 1742 both say: "The

1. John Calvin, *The Necessity of Reforming the Church* (repr., Audubon, NJ: Old Paths, 1994), 7.

acceptable way of worshiping the true God, is instituted by himself, and so limited by his own revealed will, that he may not be worshiped according to the imagination and devices of men, nor the suggestions of Satan, under any visible representations, or any other way not prescribed in the Holy Scriptures" (22.1). They also assert that "the whole counsel of God concerning all things necessary for his own glory, man's salvation, faith and life, is either expressly set down or necessarily contained in the Holy Scripture: unto which nothing at any time is to be added, whether by new revelation of the Spirit, or traditions of men. Nevertheless, we acknowledge . . . that there are some circumstances concerning the worship of God . . . common to human actions and societies, which are to be ordered by the light of nature and Christian prudence, according to the general rules of the word, which are always to be observed" (1.6). The Savoy Declaration of Faith and Order (1658), the Congregationalist emendation of the Westminster Confession (1647), affirms the same principles.

More recently, Anglican David Peterson defines worship as "an engagement with [God] *on the terms that he proposes* and in the way that he alone makes possible."[2] Even more specifically, Hughes Old, who does not employ the term *regulative principle*, nevertheless offers a description of this fundamental Reformed corporate worship principle that would have satisfied the Westminster Assembly:

> Most things we do in worship we do because God has commanded us to do them. It is because of this that we preach the gospel, we praise God in psalms and hymns, we serve God in prayer, we baptize in the name of Christ. Some things we do

---

2. David Peterson, *Engaging with God: A Biblical Theology of Worship* (Grand Rapids: Eerdmans, 1992), 20 (emphasis added).

in worship not so much because they are specifically taught in Scripture but because they are in accordance with Scripture. What is meant by that is that some of the things we do in worship we do because they are demanded by scriptural principles. For example we baptize in the name of the Father, the Son, and the Holy Spirit because this is specifically directed by Scripture. It is on the basis of scriptural principles that before the baptism we offer the Baptismal Invocation asking the Holy Spirit to fulfill inwardly what is promised in the outward sign. The basic acts of worship we perform because they are clearly commanded in Scripture. The ways and means of doing them we try to order according to scriptural principles. When something is not specifically commanded, prescribed, or directed or when there is no scriptural example to guide us in how we are to perform some particular aspect of worship we should try nevertheless to be guided by scriptural principles.[3]

What is being argued here is that there must be scriptural warrant for all we do. That warrant may come in the form of explicit directives, implicit requirements, the general principles of Scripture, positive commands, examples, and things derived from good and necessary consequences. These formulations of the Reformed approach to worship also acknowledge that lesser things about corporate worship may be decided in the absence of a specific biblical command but in accordance with faithful biblical Christian thinking under the influence of scriptural principles and sanctified reason and general revelation (e.g., whether to use bulletins, what time the services are to begin, how long they are to last, where to meet, what the ministers and congregation will wear, whether to use hymnals, how the singing is to be

3. Hughes Oliphant Old, *Worship That Is Reformed according to Scripture* (Atlanta: John Knox, 1984), 171.

led, and the like). But the first things—the central elements, the principle parts, the essentials—have a positive warrant. The incidentals and accidentals will be guided by scriptural principles.

In order to sharpen this principle and make it more perspicuous and useful, Reformed theologians speak about the substance of corporate worship (the content of its prescribed parts or elements), the elements of worship (its components or specific parts), the forms of worship (the way in which these elements of worship are carried out), and the circumstances of worship (incidental matters that of necessity demand a decision but that are not specifically commanded in the Word). Reformed theologians argue that the whole substance of worship must be biblical. Not that only words from the Bible can be used, but that all that is done and said in worship is in accordance with sound biblical theology. The content of each component must convey God's truth as revealed in his Word. They also assert that God specifically commanded the elements he desired in worship (reading the Word, preaching the Word, singing, prayer, administration of the sacraments, oaths and vows, etc.). To and from these, we may neither add nor take away. As for the form of the elements, there will be some variations: different prayers will be prayed, different songs sung, different Scriptures read and preached, the components of worship rearranged from time to time, the occasional elements (like the sacraments, oaths, and vows) performed at various chosen times, and the like. There will be, of necessity, some human discretion exercised in these matters. So here, Christian common sense under the direction of general scriptural principles, patterns, and proportions must make a determination. Finally, as to circumstances—whether we sit or stand, have pews or chairs, meet in a church building or storefront, sing from a hymnal or from memory, what time on the Lord's Day services are to be held, and more—these things must be decided upon in the absence of specific biblical direction, and hence they must be done (as with the case of the forms above) in accordance with "the light of nature and Christian prudence, according to the general rules of the word."[4]

Through the faithful implementation of this regulative principle, the various Reformed churches effected a renovation of Christianity, established a discipleship program unparalleled in Christian history, created a culture that survives to this day (albeit in a diminished scope and quality), and rejuvenated the apostolic norms of corporate worship. This chapter is a call for its deliberate reinstitution in the evangelical church as an indispensable axiom for and prerequisite to corporate worship as God intends it to be. This is a call issued by Dr. Boice when he said: "We must worship on the basis of the biblical revelation . . . [and] according to the doctrines of the Bible."[5] The key benefit of the regulative principle is that it helps to assure that God— not man—is the supreme authority for how corporate worship is to be conducted, by assuring that the Bible, God's own special revelation (and not our own opinions, tastes, likes, and theories), is the prime factor in our conduct of and approach to corporate worship.

IS THE REGULATIVE PRINCIPLE OUTMODED?

The regulative principle, however, strikes many evangelicals as outmoded. They see it as one historical expression of worship, but are not convinced that it is necessary or even applicable today. Of the more intelligent critics of this historic

4. Westminster Confession of Faith 1.6; Baptist Confession of Faith 1.6.

5. James Montgomery Boice, *Whatever Happened to the Gospel of Grace? Recovering the Doctrines That Shook the World* (Wheaton, IL: Crossway, 2001), 188.

Reformed view of worship, some view it as a solely Puritan principle: characteristic of north European culture, invented by seventeenth-century scholastic theologians, narrower than Calvin's approach, and not embraced elsewhere in the best of catholic Christianity.[6] But I want to suggest that the main reason why many evangelicals have a hard time embracing the regulative principle is that they do not believe that God tells us (or tells us much about) how to worship corporately in his Word.

Evangelicals have for a century or more been the most minimal of all the Protestants in what they think the Bible teaches us about the church in general and in their estimation of the relative importance of ecclesiology (the doctrine of the church). They do not generally believe that church government is established positively in the Word; they often do not see the local church as essential to the fulfillment of the Great Commission or to the task of Christian discipleship; they are suspicious of order as restrictive of freedom; and they generally juxtapose the priesthood of believers and local church autonomy over against the didactic authority of established church norms, confessional theology, and the testimony of the *communio sanctorum* through the ages (under Scripture). Consequently, since the doctrine of worship is a part of what the Bible teaches about the doctrine of the church, they are not predisposed in general to expect much in the way of important, definitive teaching about the conduct of corporate worship.

So, to say it again differently, the single greatest obstacle to the reform of worship in the evangelical church today is evangelicalism's general belief that New Testament Christians have few

6. This kind of criticism can be found in R. J. Gore's *Covenantal Worship: Reconsidering the Puritan Regulative Principle* (Phillipsburg, NJ: P&R Publishing, 2002) and perhaps implicitly in Tim Keller's comments in "Reformed Worship in the Global City," in *Worship by the Book*, ed. D. A. Carson (Grand Rapids: Zondervan, 2002), 193-99.

or no particular directions about how we are to worship God corporately: what elements belong in worship, what elements must always be present in well-ordered worship, what things do not belong in worship. To be even more specific, when we recall from our study of Christian ethics that every ethical action has a standard (a norm), dynamic (that which enables or empowers someone to do the action contemplated in the norm), motivation (that which impels someone to do the action), and goal (the final object[s] or purpose[s] of the action), we may say that evangelicals emphasize the dynamic of Christian worship (the grace of the Holy Spirit) and its motivation (gratitude for grace, a passion for God), but deemphasize the standard (the Bible) and goal (the prime *telos* of glorifying and enjoying God).

Evangelicals do think that worship matters, but they also often view worship as a means to some other end than that of the glorification and enjoyment of God: some view worship as evangelism (thus misunderstanding its goal); some think that a person's heart, intentions, motives, and sincerity are the only things important in how we worship (thus downplaying the Bible's standards, principles, and rules for worship); and some view the emotional product of the worship experience as the prime factor in "good" worship (thus overstressing the subjective and often unwittingly imposing particular cultural opinions about emotional expression on all worshipers). Evangelicals believe these things about worship, but they do not think that there are many biblical principles about how to worship or what we are to do and not to do in worship.

In part, this may be the result of an understandable misunderstanding of the precise nature of the discontinuity between the worship of the people of God in the old covenant and the new covenant. Evangelicals have, by and large, gotten the point of Hebrews and the rest of the New Testament on the coming of Christ as the end of the types and shadows of the elaborate

18

ceremonial worship of the old covenant. Thus they have, again rightly, rejected the approach of high church traditions (whether Roman Catholic, Eastern Orthodox, or Anglo-Catholic) that attempt to reimpose and reapply a christological version of the priestly ceremonialism of old-covenant worship or draw on the liturgical symbolism of Revelation (itself based on the worship practices of the old covenant) as normative for the church militant of the new covenant. Evangelicals know that this approach is not only confused, it is wrong and unbiblical.

Consequently, though evangelicals know that the Old Testament has instructions on what Israel was to do in worship, they tend to think that there are few if any abiding principles to be gained for Christian worship from the Old Testament, or they think that the New Testament emphases on the heart, the activity of the Holy Spirit, and worship-in-all-of-life displace these Old Testament principles, or they think that the New Testament has correspondingly little or nothing to say about the how of corporate worship, and some even think that the category of corporate worship disappears altogether in the new-covenant expression of the economy of God. But these assumptions are as wrong in one direction as high church approaches are in the other. And, not surprisingly, these assumptions help an evangelicalism enveloped in a culture of individualism, relativism, and situationalism remain, in its approach to the gathered worship of God's people, strong on the individual, weak on the corporate; strong on the subjective, weak on the objective; strong on the heart, weak on the principles.

GOD'S PERVASIVE CONCERN FOR HOW HE IS WORSHIPED

God makes it amply clear, however, throughout the Bible that he does indeed care very much about how we worship. The

Bible's answer to this query—does God care about the how of worship?—is an emphatic yes, not only in the Old Testament but also in the New Testament. Where does the Bible teach this? Obviously one place is in the detailed provisions for tabernacle worship found in Exodus 25–31, 35–40, as well as in Leviticus.

Exodus 25, for instance, in the middle of its divine instructions for the sanctuary and its furnishings, insists upon at least three aspects of the way that God's people are to worship (thus touching the standard, motivation, and goal of worship and indirectly the dynamic).

First, Israel's worship was to be willing worship. It is to be "every man whose heart moves him" (25:2) who contributes to the sanctuary (note the contrast to this in the golden-calf incident in 32:2). If worship does not spring from gratitude for God's grace, if it is not the heartfelt response to who God is and what he has done, then it is hollow.

Second, true worship (like the goal of the covenant itself) has in view spiritual communion with the living God. God orders construction of the tabernacle that he "may dwell among" his people (25:8). That is God's purpose in the old-covenant ordinances for worship, and so the people were to bear that goal in mind as they themselves built and came to the tabernacle. "I will be your God and you will be my people" is the heart and aim of the covenant—and the heart and the aim of worship. If worship aims for anything less than this, it is not worship at all but a vacuous substitute.

Third, God's worship is to be carefully ordered according to his instructions. God's initiative is prime in the design of the tabernacle (again, in contrast to the golden-calf incident). God demanded that the tabernacle and all its furnishings be made "after the pattern . . . shown to you on the mountain" (25:40). God's plan, not the people's creativity, nor even that of the artisans who would build it, was to be determinative in the making of the place where his people would meet him (and indeed, in all the actions of the priests who would serve in this worship).

This is, in essence, what the Reformers saw as a fundamental principle for Christian worship (an approach that came to be known as the regulative principle). This principle, in short, states that worship in its content, motivation, and aim is to be determined by God alone. He teaches us how to think about him and how to approach him. The further we get away, then, from his directions the less we actually worship.

But many fine evangelical theologians object at this point and say: "Yes, this principle was true for tabernacle worship, but not for new-covenant worship." The idea behind this objection is that because of its unique typological significance, Old Testament tabernacle worship was guarded by unique requirements that God did not apply elsewhere in the Old Testament or in the New Testament to the corporate worship of his people. So, they say, though our worship should be guided by biblical principles (in the same way as is the rest of life), it is not restricted to that which is positively warranted by the Word (as was tabernacle worship).[7]

However, the Bible, the whole Bible, contradicts this position. The emphasis on God's concern for the how of worship (in its standard, motivation, dynamic, and goal) is pervasive, not only in the ceremonial code, but also in the moral law, not only in the Pentateuch but also in the Prophets, not only in the Old Testament but also in the New, not only in Paul but also in Jesus's teaching. Consider the following.

---

7. John Frame makes this kind of an argument (though not as radically as others, it should be said) in *Worship in Spirit and Truth* (Phillipsburg, NJ: P&R Publishing, 1996), esp. xii-xiii, 44-45.

The Account of Cain and Abel

At the very beginnings of special revelation, integral to the post-fall story of the seed of the woman and the seed of the serpent, is found the account of Cain and Abel (Gen. 4:3–8). Abel offers "the firstlings of his flock and of their fat portions" and Cain offers "the fruit of the ground," but the Lord "had regard for Abel and for his offering; but for Cain and for his offering He had no regard." Why? Well, the narrative is sparse but suggestive of the answer. The Lord's rebuke ("if you do well, will not your countenance be lifted up?") coupled with the stated contrast between the brothers' respective offerings indicates that Cain's offering was either deficient according the standard of God's requirements (and what they were is not spelled out for us, unless Moses expects his readers to think proleptically) or that his heart attitude/motivation in making the offering was deficient. In other words, Cain failed to worship in either spirit or truth or both. The how of worship was lacking in either its standard or motivation, and so God rejected his worship.

Thus, at the outset of revelation, in a section of Genesis replete with emphases about the beginnings of worship and its importance, God sets forth a warning to every reader and hearer that he is very particular about how his people approach him in worship. It is before the moral law is expounded at Sinai. It is in no way connected to the tabernacle worship of Exodus or to the levitical system. It tells us before those things are ever announced that God cares about the how of worship.

The Story of the Exodus

Grounded in the great redemptive story of the exodus is another principle that shows the exceeding importance that God attaches to corporate worship and thus moves us to a concern for the how of worship. For instance, the whole exodus account, especially from Exodus 3:12 on, stresses that God's people are redeemed in order that they might worship him. Moses's very call emphasizes that God sends Moses to Egypt to deliver his people that they might worship him.

Listen to the reiterated emphases of these passages: "When you have brought the people out of Egypt, you shall worship" (Ex. 3:12); "let us go a three days' journey into the wilderness, that we may sacrifice to the LORD our God" (3:18); "let My son go that he may serve [or worship] Me" (4:23); "let My people go that they may celebrate a feast to Me in the wilderness" (5:1); "let us go a three days' journey into the wilderness that we may sacrifice to the LORD our God" (5:3).

Do not underestimate this repeated language. This is not merely a ruse to get Pharaoh to temporarily release the children of Israel. It is the primary reason why God sets his people free: to worship him. The primacy of worship in a believer's life is thus set forth. We are saved to worship!

These passages, of course, reflect an interest in both worship in all of life and the specific activity of corporate worship. However, the highlighting of the specific activity of corporate worship in Moses's language and teaching about worship in the era of pre-tabernacle worship in Exodus (i.e., in his differentiation of the two types of worship [gathered praise and life service], in his description of the specific content of that gathered worship, in his interest in the initial location of that gathered worship [the mountain that God had shown], in the inclusion of stipulations on corporate worship in the moral law, in his heavily emphasized accounts of the subsequent abuse of corporate worship in the rebellion of the golden calf, and more) teaches us to be circumspect in our approach to corporate worship.

The First and Second Commandments

Grounded in the moral law itself and revealed in the first and second commandments (Ex. 20:2–6) is a fundamental

23

indication that God is concerned not only with the whom of corporate worship, but also the how of corporate worship. No matter how these commands are numbered, the text still makes both points!

> I am the LORD your God, who brought you out of the land of Egypt, out of the house of slavery. You shall have no other gods before Me. You shall not make for yourself an idol, or any likeness of what is in heaven above or on the earth beneath or in the water under the earth. You shall not worship them or serve them; for I, the LORD your God, am a jealous God, visiting the iniquity of the fathers on the children, on the third and the fourth generations of those who hate Me, but showing lovingkindness to thousands, to those who love Me and keep My commandments.

God indicates here not only that he alone is to be worshiped, but also that he is not to be worshiped via images. Additionally, he stresses his extreme sensitivity about these matters. The very mention of the use of images anchors this passage in a concern for corporate worship (although, of course, it has implications for worship in all of life). This text, expressing the eternal and abiding moral law and not merely the ceremonial system of the tabernacle is the very foundation of the Reformed concern for "carefulness in worship." Because God indicates that he is jealous about the whom and the how of worship, we are to be exceeding careful about the whom and the how of worship, and the best way to do that is to follow the regulative principle.

The ten words themselves are a disclosure of God's own nature and not merely a revelation of temporary social, religious, and moral norms. The first command shows us a Lord who alone is God. The second witnesses to a God who is sovereign even in the way we relate to him (since there he teaches us that we may neither think about him nor worship him according to our own human categories and designs, but must rather know him and glorify him on his own terms and by his own revelation). Because these commands teach us first and foremost about what God is like, they also provide for us permanent direction on how we are to think of God, how we are to worship God, and that God cares greatly about how we think of and worship him.

Three points arise from a careful consideration of the second command.

God's Word must govern our knowledge of God, and thus its governance of worship is vital. Divine revelation must control our idea of God, but since worship contributes to our idea of God, the only way that God's revelation can remain foremost in our thinking about God is if God's revelation also controls our worship of God. God's self-disclosure, his self-revelation, is to dominate our conception of him, and therefore God's people are not to make images of God or the gods: "You shall not make for yourself an idol, or any likeness of what is in heaven above or on the earth beneath or in the water under the earth." An idol or graven image or carved image refers, literally, to something hacked or chiseled into a likeness. Thus the command demands that there is to be no image representation of God in Israel. The phraseology of Exodus 20:4 indicates that there is to be no image-making of God or gods for any reason. This prohibition clearly extends to images of other gods, as well as to images of the one true God. Deuteronomy 4:15–18 says:

> So watch yourselves carefully, *since you did not see any form on the day the Lord spoke to you* at Horeb from the midst of the fire, so that you do not act corruptly and make a graven image for yourselves in the form of any figure, the likeness of male

or female, the likeness of any animal that is on the earth, the likeness of any winged bird that flies in the sky, the likeness of anything that creeps on the ground, the likeness of any fish that is in the water below the earth.

This moral law expressly teaches us that the Bible is to be our rule for how we corporately worship and even think about God. The Bible (God's own self-disclosure and revelation)—not our own innovations, imaginations, experiences, opinions, and representations—is to be the source of our idea of God. By the way, this is why Protestant houses of worship have historically been plain, bereft of overt religious symbolism and certainly without representations of deity. The Bible is to be central in forming our image of God and informing our worship of him. And since the how of corporate worship contributes to our image of God, it is exceedingly important that we worship in accordance with the Bible. Jewish commentator Nahum Sarna expresses the force of the second command this way:

> The forms of worship are now regulated. The revolutionary Israelite concept of God entails His being wholly separate from the world of His creation and wholly other than what the human mind can conceive or the human imagination depict. Therefore, any material representation of divinity is prohibited, a proscription elaborated in Deuteronomy 4:12, 15–19, where it is explained that the people heard "the sound of words" at Sinai "but perceived no shape—nothing but a voice." In the Israelite view any [humanly initiated] symbolic representation of God must necessarily be both inadequate and a distortion, for an image becomes identified with what it represents and is soon looked upon as the place and presence of the Deity. In the end the image itself will become the locus of reverence and an object of worship, all of which constitutes

the complete nullification of the singular essence of Israelite monotheism.[8]

But there is even more to be said about the underlying rationale of the second commandment. Again we ask, Why is there to be no image-making in Israel? Marshall McLuhan's famous dictum that "the medium is the message" sparks this interesting observation by Neil Postman:

The clearest way to see through a culture is to attend to its tools for conversation. I might add that my interest in this point of view was first stirred by a prophet far more formidable than McLuhan, more ancient than Plato. In studying the Bible as a young man, I found intimations of the idea that forms of media favor particular kinds of content and therefore are capable of taking command of a culture. I refer specifically to the Decalogue, the Second Commandment of which prohibits the Israelites from making concrete images of anything [as a representation of God]. "Thou shalt not make unto thee any graven image, any likeness of any thing that is in heaven above, or that is in the earth beneath, or that is in the water beneath the earth." I wondered then, as so many others have, as to why the God of these people would have included instructions on how they were to symbolize, or not symbolize, their experience [of him]. It is a strange injunction to include as part of an ethical system unless its author assumed a connection between forms of human communication and the quality of a culture. We may hazard a guess that a people who are being asked to embrace an abstract, universal deity would be rendered unfit to do so by the habit of drawing pictures or making

8. Nahum M. Sarna, *The JPS Torah Commentary: Exodus* (Philadelphia: Jewish Publication Society, 1991), 110. My addition in brackets.

statues or depicting their ideas [of him] in any concrete, iconographic forms. The God of the Jews was to exist in the Word and through the Word, an unprecedented conception requiring the highest order of abstract thinking. Iconography thus became blasphemy so that a new kind of God could enter a culture. People like ourselves who are in the process of converting their culture from word-centered to image-centered might profit by reflecting on this Mosaic injunction.[9]

Thus, because Israel's view of God, its understanding of God was to be controlled by his self-revelation and by not human imagination or representation, therefore its worship was to be aniconic—without images and visible representation of deity—because the how of worship contributes significant components to our conception of God. That means, of course, that Christian worship, too, is to be aniconic. We expand on this thought in a second point of consideration.

God's own character and Word must govern our worship of God. God's nature and revelation are to control our worship of him, and therefore God's people are not to worship images of other gods or worship the true God through images: "You shall not worship them or serve them" (Ex. 20:5a). This phrase further specifies that graven images are to be neither worshiped or served. Yes, of course, false gods are not to be served/worshiped (which is obviously entailed in the first command), but even more to the point—the one true God is not to be served/worshiped through the use of images. This very point is driven home in the stories of the golden calf (Ex. 32:1–5) and the idolatry of Jeroboam (1 Kings 12:28).

9. Neil Postman, *Amusing Ourselves to Death* (New York: Penguin, 1985), 8-9. My addition in brackets.

This command is obviously directly relevant to the use of images in worship and devotion in Roman Catholicism and Eastern Orthodoxy and even in branches of Protestantism (we must now sadly say). Still, we may venture that the greatest violations of this in our time are nonvisual, but rather mental and volitional. When people say things like, "Well, I know the Bible says that, but I like to think of God as . . ." they are no less idolatrous in their thinking, and thus worshiping, than was Israel at the foot of Sinai on that fateful day of spiritual adultery with the calf.

In contrast to all human creativity and initiative, the Bible is to be our rule for how we worship God, because the Bible is our rule for how we are to think about God—and how we worship in turn impacts our concept of God. Put another way: how we worship determines whom we worship. That is why both the medium and the message, both the means and the object, must be attended to in true worship. So, the Bible (God's own revelation regarding himself and his worship)—and not our own innovations, imaginations, experiences, opinions, and representations—is to determine how we worship God.

This reminds us that there are two ways to commit idolatry: worship something other than the true God or worship the true God in the wrong way. And the second word of the moral law speaks to them both. In fact, the second commandment disallows three things: making images of either false gods or the true God; using humanly initiated (unwarranted) images in worship; and, by extension, using means or media other than those by which God has appointed us to worship. Our Puritan ancestors called these innovations in corporate worship "will-worship." Not surprisingly, then, the second commandment is one of the biblical sources of what the Reformers called the regulative principle. Terry Johnson puts it this way: "In prohibiting worship through images, God declares that He alone determines how He is to be worshiped. Though their use be ever so sincere and sensible (as aids to worship) images are not pleasing to Him, and by implication, *neither is anything else that He has not sanctioned.*"[10]

God's seriousness about worship is displayed in his threats against deviation from his Word. The importance of the manner and purity of our worship is seen from God's nature, warnings, and promises as expressed in the second command, and so God's people are to refrain from this because of who God is and because of what he warns and promises. Exodus 20:5b—6 reads: "For I, the LORD your God, am a jealous God, visiting the iniquity of the fathers on the children, on the third and the fourth generations of those who hate Me, but showing lovingkindness to thousands, to those who love Me and keep My commandments." The character of God is presented here in a way shocking to our tolerance-drenched culture. He is jealous. He refuses to share his glory or his worship with anything or anyone else. The expression itself is an anthropopathism (an ascription of human emotional qualities to God), but it is linguistically or philologically an anthropomorphism (an ascription of human physical qualities to God): the older meaning of the word behind the term *jealous* or *impassioned* is that God is "to become red."[11] Alan Cole helps us appreciate the force of this kind of idiom in forming our understanding of the character of God:

> Like "love" and "hate" in the Old Testament (Mai. 1:2, 3), "jealousy" does not refer to an emotion so much as to an activity, in this case an activity of violence and vehemence, that springs from the rupture of a personal bond as exclusive

10. Terry Johnson, *Reformed Worship: Worship That Is according to Scripture* (Greenville, SC: Reformed Academic Press, 2000), 24 (emphasis original).
11. See Sarna, *Exodus*, 110.

as that of the marriage bond. This is not therefore to be seen as intolerance but exclusiveness, and it springs both from the uniqueness of God (who is not one among many) and the uniqueness of His relationship to Israel. No husband who truly loved his wife could endure to share her with another man: no more will God share Israel with a rival.[12]

The idiom, the expression, is obvious. God is calling to our minds the righteous jealousy of a husband wronged. Sarna puts it just right: "a jealous God" is "a rendering that understands the marriage bond to be the implied metaphor for the covenant between God and His people . . . . It underscores the vigorous, intensive, and punitive nature of the divine response to apostasy and to modes of worship unacceptable to Himself."[13] In other words, God is saying in this warning, "My people, if you commit spiritual adultery in your worship, I will righteously respond like the most fearsome wronged husband you have ever known." The discontinuities between divine and human behavior are assumed and implicit in the idiom, but the point is crystal clear. Betray God by idolatry, which is spiritual adultery, and he will deal with you like a red-eyed, jilted spouse.

Here again, then, we see further grounds for the Reformed doctrine of carefulness in worship. The strictness of his justice mentioned here, that he punishes sin indefatigably, only adds to that concern for carefulness. It is fascinating to note the language: those who are idolatrous hate God and that those who worship according to his commands love him. The respective meanings of "hate" (to disobey) and "love" (to obey) need to be appreciated here. This all adds up to stress that the way we

12. R. Alan Cole, *Exodus: An Introduction and Commentary* (Leicester, UK: IVP, 1973), 156.
13. Sarna, *Exodus*, 110.

31

worship or, more specifically, the way in which we follow his commands for worship, is a reflection of our knowledge of God and how seriously we take him.

One reason that "Sing the Bible, pray the Bible, read the Bible, preach the Bible" is a motto for worship in my own congregation is out of respect for this command. We strive to be sure that all that we sing is scriptural, that our prayers are saturated with Scripture, that much of the Word of God is read in each public service, and that the preaching is based on the Bible—in order that we might honor the one true God and not some idol of our own invention. The Bible supplies the substance of and direction for our worship and thus provides the surest way to know who God is and what he is like.

The Story of the Golden Calf

Grounded in the trauma of the incident with the golden calf (Ex. 32–34) is yet another testimony to the sheer importance of the how of worship. If there is any lesson here at all, it is that we cannot take the worship of God into our own hands, for Israel's rebellion against the moral law's commands regarding worship is presented here as a breaking of the covenant and a rejection of God. It is vital to remember that this is not a defection from the ceremonial law or the worship of the tabernacle—the people had not yet received these. Moses presents the actions of Israel as a contradiction of moral law. Hence, this story has special abiding significance. Several huge themes are operating at once in this section of Exodus. Among others, this whole section highlights the doctrine of sin. It is a "fall story"—the story of Israel's covenant-breaking. We find a summary of this defection in Exodus 32:1–6:

> Now when the people saw that Moses delayed to come down
> from the mountain, the people assembled about Aaron and

said to him, "Come, make us a god who will go before us; as for this Moses, the man who brought us up from the land of Egypt, we do not know what has become of him." Aaron said to them, "Tear off the gold rings which are in the ears of your wives, your sons, and your daughters, and bring them to me." Then all the people tore off the gold rings which were in their ears and brought them to Aaron. He took this from their hand, and fashioned it with a graving tool and made it into a molten calf; and they said, "This is your god, O Israel, who brought you up from the land of Egypt." Now when Aaron saw this, he built an altar before it; and Aaron made a proclamation and said, "Tomorrow shall he a feast to the LORD." So the next day they rose early and offered burnt offerings, and brought peace offerings; and the people sat down to eat and to drink, and rose up to play.

Israel, impatient at Moses's long delay, comes to Aaron not only looking for a visible representation of deity or of the divine presence, but essentially looking for a new mediator (there is a sense in which the golden calf and Aaron serve as their chosen replacements for Moses). The people's request seems to be not a request for a different god, a god other than Yahweh, but rather a representation of him (or of the mediator). The people also speak disrespectfully and dismissively of Moses, God's hand-picked mediator. Ironically, without him and his subsequent intercession, they would have all perished here! Their demand of Aaron, to make a graven image (whatever interpretation is put on it with regard to its violation of the first or second commandments), is astonishing.

Aaron facilitates their requests. Why he does so, we are not told, but he does not come out of this narrative favorably. Some of the spoils of the Egyptians are used to create the idol, and the rebellion was widespread ("all the people"). Aaron makes a golden young bull or ox idol (was it a shadowing of Apis or the Canaanite deities or a proleptic foreshadowing of the idolatry of Jeroboam?) and identifies it with or as the God who brought them up from Egypt. Some commentators suggest that the young bull was the pedestal on which the invisible God of Israel was standing, while others argue that it was a representation of deity. Either way, it is a violation of the second command! In some ways, the suggestion that the idol is a representation of the mediator even further strengthens the traditional Reformed interpretation of this passage and the second command.

Now that a "do-it-yourself god" or representation of him or material mediatorial object of his presence has been made, Aaron proceeds to make a do-it-yourself altar/sanctuary/place of worship and encounter. He still insists, however, that this is the worship of the Lord, that is, the true God, which suggests that Moses is highlighting a defection from the second command in this story. The feast day comes, the people worship their self-derived god in their self-derived way, and gross immorality results. Idolatry leads to immorality. This is the chain of connection in false worship: wrong worship, which is impiety, leads to immorality. Cole says: "This is not a casual incident: it is an organized cult, with a statue, altar, priest and festival."[14]

One even wonders if this could have been a deliberate reaction against the aniconic worship announced in the ten words by those who had become accustomed to iconic worship through years in Egypt. Syncretism or pluralism or both was a part of what was going on in the camp of Israel. It was syncretism in that some in Israel wanted to worship the God of Israel in a pagan way (in this case, through visible representation), though God's command made clear that Israel's worship was to be exclusively aniconic. If there was pluralism at work in the

14. Cole, *Exodus*, 215.

incident, it involved worshiping someone or something along-side of or in addition to Yahweh, which is also idolatry.

Whatever the case, the whole passage points up (again) that how we worship is very important to God. Several applications flow from this principle and its violation in the golden-calf event:

- impatience with God's timing is an enemy of faith;
- we cannot choose our own mediator;
- we cannot picture the true God as we wish or will;
- we cannot worship the true God and something else;
- we cannot worship the true God except in the way he commands; and
- false worship leads to false living and immorality.

Cole perceptively notes: "It is because Israel is so like us in every way that the stories of Israel have such exemplary value (1 Cor. 10)."[15] Terence Fretheim offers striking insights on the whole incident of the golden calf:

At every key point the people's building project contrasts with the tabernacle that God has just announced. This gives to the account a heavy ironic cast. (1) The people seek to create what God has already provided; (2) they, rather than God, take the initiative; (3) offerings are demanded rather than willingly presented; (4) the elaborate preparations are missing alto-gether; (5) the painstaking length of time needed for building becomes an overnight rush job; (6) the careful provision for guarding the presence of the Holy One turns into an open-air object of immediate accessibility; (7) the invisible, intangible God becomes a visible, tangible image; and (8) the personal,

---

15. Cole, 212.

active God becomes an impersonal object that cannot see or speak or act. The ironic effect is that the people forfeit the very divine presence they had hoped to bind more closely to themselves. At the heart of the matter, the most important of the commandments had been violated.[16]

God's verdict in Exodus 32:7–10 only reinforces this:

> Then the LORD spoke to Moses, "Go down at once, for your people, whom you brought up from the land of Egypt, have corrupted themselves. They have quickly turned aside from the way which I commanded them. They have made for themselves a molten calf, and have worshiped it and have sacrificed to it and said, 'This is your god, O Israel, who brought you up from the land of Egypt!'" The LORD said to Moses, "I have seen this people, and behold, they are an obstinate people. Now then let Me alone, that My anger may burn against them and that I may destroy them; and I will make of you a great nation."

God knows what is going on even though Moses does not, so he tells Moses to go see for himself. God uses the language of disownment here—"whom *you* brought up." It is also ironic in light of the people's disowning words about Moses in verse 1. God nails them in their crime accurately and specifically. They have:

- *quickly* (through impatience)
- *turned aside from the way* (i.e., forsaken their covenant obligations of living in the Lord's way of life),

16. Terence E. Fretheim, *Exodus*, Interpretation (Louisville: John Knox, 1991), 280-81.

- *which he commanded them* (i.e., they have broken the covenant directives);
- more specifically, they have done this by *making and worshiping an idol* (in contradiction of the first and second commands)
- and by *claiming it to be the saving God of Israel* (thus demeaning the one true God).

It is important to note that, in his accusatory language ("they have quickly turned aside *from the way which I commanded them*"), God charges Israel not with departing from him, but from his way, his commands about worship (which consequently means a departure from God himself). Sarna notes, "Significantly, the text does not say 'from Me'; they have adopted pagan modes of worship, but in worship of the God of Israel."[17] This whole indictment emphasizes the importance of the how of worship. Violation of God's commands on worship is viewed as breaking the covenant and is cataclysmic in its consequences. Israel deserved to be disowned and cut off. That is why "before the Hebrews were allowed to erect the sanctuary and to worship in it, they had to repent of their sin and undergo a covenant renewal."[18]

We have now seen four old-covenant examples of the Bible's concern about the how of corporate worship. None of them are tied to the ceremonial code or to tabernacle worship. But Christians may be anxious to know if the New Testament really has testimony to this concern, and so we hasten on, leaving behind dozens of Old Testament passages that corroborate our claims, among them the following:

17. Sarna, *Exodus*, 204.
18. John Currid, *Exodus* (Darlington, UK: Evangelical Press, 2001), 2:268.

- *The story of Nadab and Abihu* (Lev. 10), who offer up "strange fire" to the Lord, that is, making an offering in a manner "which He had not commanded them" (10:1), and God strikes them dead (10:2). Moses records a thundering axiom in God's verdict: "By those who come near Me I will be treated as holy" (10:3).
- *The warnings of Deuteronomy* (4:2; 12:32) that stress God's demand that whatever he commands, especially in worship, "you shall be careful to do; you shall not add to nor take away from it."
- *God's rejection of Saul's unprescribed worship* (1 Sam. 15:22): when Saul offered a sacrifice out of accord with God's instructions, he was rebuked with "to obey is better than sacrifice."
- *The story of David and Uzzah and the ark*, which explicitly indicates that David knew he had violated the regulative principle of worship (2 Sam. 6, especially vv. 3, 13).
- *God's rejection of pagan rites in Jeremiah's day*, "which I never commanded or spoke of, nor did it ever enter My mind" (Jer. 19:5; 32:35).

Jesus's Rejection of Pharisaic Worship

Grounded in Jesus's rejection of Pharisaic worship (Matt. 15:1–14), we find a dominical, new-covenant reassertion of the importance of the way in which we worship. Jesus cares about the how of worship. This passage is easily and often misunderstood, precisely because we live in an antitraditional age (where "new" generally means "good"). We tend to view the Pharisees as being overly scrupulous in their study and application of God's law. Jesus, however, never makes that charge against them. His critique is always in another direction. It is their laxity about God's law and their tenuous casuistry that undermined the prime force of moral law and drew his ire. Matthew's text is a picture of the human-made ritual of the religion of the Pharisees:

> Then some Pharisees and scribes came to Jesus from Jerusalem and said, "Why do Your disciples break the tradition of the elders? For they do not wash their hands when they eat bread." And He answered and said to them, "Why do you yourselves transgress the commandment of God for the sake of your tradition? For God said, 'Honor your father and mother,' and, 'He who speaks evil of father or mother is to be put to death.' But you say, 'Whoever says to his father or mother, "Whatever I have that would help you has been given to God," he is not to honor his father or his mother.' And by this you invalidated the word of God for the sake of your tradition. You hypocrites, rightly did Isaiah prophesy of you:
>
> > 'This people honors Me with their lips,
> > But their heart is far away from Me.
> > But in vain do they worship Me,
> > Teaching as doctrines the precepts of men.'"
>
> After Jesus called the crowd to Him, He said to them, "Hear and understand. It is not what enters into the mouth that defiles the man, but what proceeds out of the mouth, this defiles the man."
>
> Then the disciples came and said to Him, "Do You know that the Pharisees were offended when they heard this statement?" But He answered and said, "Every plant which My heavenly Father did not plant shall be uprooted. Let them alone; they are blind guides of the blind. And if a blind man guides a blind man, both will fall into a pit."

In this passage, the Pharisees bring a charge against Jesus that he allowed his disciples to break the "tradition of the elders" regarding ritual handwashing. This handwashing was not hygienic, but religious. Note that it is Jesus who particularly applies the issue to the matter of the act of worship.

Tradition in the New Testament can be either positive (2 Thess. 2:15; 3:6) or negative (Mark 7:3, 9, 13; Col. 2:8; 1 Peter 1:18), depending on the context. Here it refers to the traditions of the elders, which involved:

- very high estimation of the specific interpretations and applications of the Torah by the elders, even approaching the point of these views and deductions being considered to be equally binding as the law of God itself;
- not only applications of the law of God that went beyond what the law of itself taught, but often went beyond it in the wrong direction; and
- interpretations and applications of the law that failed to do justice to certain central moral requirements of the law (focusing, rather, on the ceremonial/ritual).

This exchange on the issue of the tradition gives Jesus the opportunity to discuss the important matter of ceremonial versus moral defilement and, ultimately, that of worship.

Jesus, using a phrase that precisely parallels the charge of the Pharisees, responds by charging them with breaking God's commandment. He then juxtaposes God's commandment with a practice that they have invented or endorsed: the rule of *korban*. Jesus's charge against them is that they have undercut the authority of God's Word in preference for human-made rules. They have taken away from the Word by adding to it. Their teaching is "subtraction by addition." Jesus illustrates that the Pharisees have a fundamental misunderstanding and foster a misuse of the ceremonial code in relation to the moral law (Matt. 15:3–6); and his verdict is that this misunderstanding/ misuse stems from a hypocritical heart (15:7–9).

It is important to note that Jesus does not critique the Pharisees for being too tied to old-fashioned practices, caring about what the Torah says too much, or being too nitpicky about God's law. He charges them with ignoring God's law and attacking God's law by adding to it! Indeed, Jesus says that the words of Isaiah are perfectly suited to describe the Pharisees' worship:

- it is *lip service* rather than God-honoring, in which their hearts are far away from him, rather than truly loving him;
- it is *empty worship*, mere form; and
- it is *human-made*, not based on the prescriptions of the Word.

Note then that Jesus's critique is internal and external: it pertains to both the heart and to the outward obedience of God's Word. It has definite application to "all-of-life worship," but also to corporate worship. Indeed, the parallel account in Mark 7 makes explicit what is implicit in Matthew. Jesus's teaching here has enormous significance for Christian corporate worship in relation to the ceremonial law. Mark 7:19 tells us that Jesus's words meant the abolition of the ceremonial code's food laws for all new-covenant believers. The Book of Hebrews, based upon the underlying rationale of the abolition of the food laws (which was the dominical fulfillment of the totality of the ceremonial system), applies this same principle to show that we are no longer to worship corporately via the ceremonial/ sacrificial forms of old-covenant corporate worship. Back to our immediate point though, Jesus makes it amply clear here that he cares about the how of worship, about the heart and obedience to the Word, not only in worship in all of life, but in the corporate praise we bring.

Jesus's Words to the Woman at the Well

We find in Jesus's words to the Samaritan woman (John 4:20–26) an indication of the importance of the how of worship for new-covenant believers. In this deeply moving account of Jesus's encounter with the woman at the well, after his uncovering of her hidden sin and shame, she asks him about a worship matter of long dispute between Jews and Samaritans and of great importance to them both:

> "Our fathers worshiped in this mountain, and you people say that in Jerusalem is the place where men ought to worship." Jesus said to her, "Woman, believe Me, an hour is coming when neither in this mountain nor in Jerusalem will you worship the Father. You worship what you do not know; we worship what we know, for salvation is from the Jews. But an hour is coming, and now is, when the true worshipers will worship the Father in spirit and truth; for such people the Father seeks to be His worshipers. God is spirit, and those who worship Him must worship in spirit and truth." The woman said to Him, "I know that Messiah is coming (He who is called Christ); when that One comes, He will declare all things to us." Jesus said to her, "I who speak to you am He."

Jesus's answer thunders with points of significance regarding the momentous redemptive-historical transition that he was effecting in his own life, ministry, death, and resurrection; but it also speaks specifically to numerous principles of corporate worship that remain essential for Christians today. We point to but three of them here.

Jesus indicates a redemptive historical shift regarding the place of worship. For hundreds of years, the divinely appointed site for sacrificial worship had been in Jerusalem. This was the only place where the acts of worship, originally authorized in the giving of the tabernacle structure and ordinances in Exodus, were to be done. It was the focal point of the manifestation of the presence of God with Israel. In response, however, to the woman's query whether to worship in this mountain or in Jerusalem, Jesus begins by stressing that "an hour is coming when neither in this mountain nor in Jerusalem will you worship the Father."

In other words, in a sentence Jesus indicates a time not far in the future in which the old-covenant place for tabernacle/temple/ceremonial/sacrificial worship would no longer have relevance for the true believer. In that hour, which came through his resurrection and ascension and Pentecostal affusion of the Spirit, the place of worship is no longer geographical but ecclesial. Wherever believers gather in his name will be the place of worship: "For where two or three have gathered together in My name, I am there in their midst" (Matt. 18:20). The house in which his presence is known is the house of his people, whatever physical structure they may find themselves in. This is one reason the Reformers shut and locked their church doors (outside of corporate worship times): to stress that no place or building held peculiar spiritual significance and value. This is a new-covenant principle of worship—it is not tied to any specific location. The Westminster Confession expresses this teaching of Jesus this way:

> Neither prayer, nor any other part of religious worship, is now, under the gospel, either tied unto, or made more acceptable by any place in which it is performed, or towards which it is directed: but God is to be worshiped everywhere, in spirit and truth; as in private families daily, and in secret each one by

himself, so more solemnly in the public assemblies, which are not carelessly or willfully to be neglected or forsaken when God, by his word or providence, calls thereunto. (21.6)

Jesus stresses that worship is response to revelation and thus must be according to revelation. Jesus's answer "neither in this mountain nor in Jerusalem" was not all he had to say in response to what was, in effect, a query about the legitimacy of Samaritan worship. He went on to say, "You worship what you do not know; we worship what we know, for salvation is from the Jews." In other words, the Samaritans were wrong to worship in their own self-chosen place. And because their worship was not in accord with God's revelation, they were also confused about whom they were worshiping.

Jesus's words here are a confirmation that the Old Testament's teaching on the central significance of the tabernacle/temple worship had been rightly understood by Israel and that any departure from it (precisely because it would entail a departure from the commands of God's revelation) would lead worshipers, no matter how sincere, into confusion about God. Israel knew its God because it worshiped him according to his revelation; but because the Samaritans did not worship according to revelation, they did not know their God. This is a new-covenant example of the maxim "how you worship determines what you become." This is why Jesus later says that worship must be "in truth." True worship is impossible for the Samaritans (and for us) as long as they devise their own worship.

Jesus reemphasizes the importance of worship in the new-covenant era. He says: "An hour is coming, and now is, when the true worshipers will worship the Father in spirit and truth; for such people the Father seeks to be His worshipers." To glorify and enjoy God, to meet with God and engage with him, is so important to him that he himself is *seeking* us to become his worshipers. No higher commendation of the colossal importance of the activity of worship for new-covenant believers is imaginable. The plural *worshipers* indicates not only the scope of the future kingdom but also the corporate, congregational nature of the worship that God seeks. More, much more could be said, but this suffices to show that far from being unconcerned about the how of worship in the new covenant, Jesus himself labored to stress the vital importance of how we go about worshiping God.

Paul's Rejection of the Colossian Heresy

Grounded in Paul's rejection of the Colossian heresy (Col. 2:16–19) is yet another reminder that in the new-covenant era the how of worship still matters very much. Without even considering his strong rejection of the ethical teaching of the errorists, it is obvious that Paul was responding to false teaching on worship in Colossae: "Therefore no one is to act as your judge in regard to food or drink or in respect to a festival or a new moon or a Sabbath day—things which are a mere shadow of what is to come; but the substance belongs to Christ."

Paul here emphatically calls on Christians not to allow people to judge them according to or influence them into following human-made or abrogated old-covenant rituals, even the old-covenant seventh-day Sabbath. Nothing he says here denigrates the new-covenant Lord's Day in any way; the religious activities he mentions in 2:16 are all parts of old-covenant worship, no longer binding on the new-covenant Christian. Paul is simply reminding Christians that they are not under the ceremonial law. And he sees that as vital for right corporate worship among new covenant Christians. His words still speak today to those who long for the elaborate liturgical and symbolical worship of the old covenant. Do not pass by the substance to return to the shadows, he says. So this response of Paul has to do with understanding the discontinuities of redemptive history.

Then Paul takes on angel worship and the false humility that accompanies it: "Let no one keep defrauding you of your prize by delighting in self-abasement and the worship of the angels, taking his stand on visions he has seen, inflated without cause by his fleshly mind, and not holding fast to the head, from whom the entire body, being supplied and held together by the joints and ligaments, grows with a growth which is from God." His critique is a rejection of the visions on which such worship is based and a condemnation of the insufficient view of Christ inherently entailed in such an activity.

The criticism also clearly pertains to corporate worship, at least in part. It is hard to imagine such a thing as "angel worship in all of life" no matter what one does with the notoriously difficult phrase *the worship of angels!*[19] Furthermore, the wrongheadedness of this worship has to do not merely with the internal and the subjective, but the external and the objective. Yes, Paul hints at heart insincerity in his comments about self-abasement juxtaposed with self-inflation, but his main points are that (1) the worship is not God-commanded but human-originated and (2) the worship does not do justice to the person and exaltation of Christ or our union with him. It is from this passage that the wise old Puritan divines got their phrase *will-worship*. Worshiping according to our ideas, however sincere, is an act of

---

19. R. P. Martin says, "In some way veneration must have been paid to the angels as part of the cultic apparatus of this religion." *Colossians and Philemon*, New Century Bible Commentary (Grand Rapids: Eerdmans, 1973), 94. I am well aware of the herculean efforts of modern Reformed critics of the regulative principle to make this passage inapplicable to corporate worship, but Paul's contextual discussion is fatal to their design. What has Paul just been talking about? Baptism! The whole section contains allusions to the practice of public worship.

self-worship and specifically the worship of our own wills and wants. Here, once again, we find the New Testament far from unconcerned about the how of worship. For Paul it was vital, a fact even more apparent (if that is possible) in the next passage.

Paul's Directives for Corinth

Grounded in Paul's phenomenal directives for genuine charismatic worship in Corinth (1 Cor. 14) is an unparalleled expression of the new-covenant importance of the way in which we worship. Paul is perfectly willing to regulate the form and content of charismatic worship founded in the real and powerful working of the third person of the Trinity, God the Holy Spirit! Whatever we believe about the continuation of revelation, tongues, prophecy, and the like, this passage (in spite of its extreme interpretive challenges) yields crystal-clear teaching on numerous points relating to corporate worship, which are applicable to all Christians in all ages.

Paul places a premium on corporate worship that is understandable and mutually edifying. Hence, he values prophecy above uninterpreted tongues precisely because prophecy edifies the church:

> For one who speaks in a tongue does not speak to men but to God. . . . But one who prophesies speaks to men for edification and exhortation and consolation. One who speaks in a[n uninterpreted] tongue edifies himself; but one who prophesies edifies the church. Now I wish that you all spoke in tongues, but even more that you would prophesy; and greater is one who prophesies than one who speaks in tongues, unless he interprets, so that the church may receive edifying. (1 Cor. 14:2–5)

The edification that Paul contemplates is rooted in the mind, the understanding, and mature thinking. The vocabulary for this is apparent throughout. So edification, comprehensibility, the centrality of preaching, and the purpose in preaching to address the understanding and conscience, far from being cultural preferences derived from post-Renaissance, north-European rationalism, are instead apostolic principles or characteristics of new-covenant worship that trump even extraordinary activities enabled by God the Holy Spirit.

Paul describes apostolic-era corporate worship. Simply using Paul's vocabulary and phrases, we can build a description of the components and character of charismatic, apostolic-era corporate worship:

- spiritual gifts (v. 1)
- prophecy (v. 6)
- tongues (v. 5 and elsewhere)
- edification, exhortation, and consolation (v. 3)
- interpretation (v. 26)
- revelation, knowledge, and teaching (v. 6)
- meaning (v. 10)
- prayer and singing with the mind (v. 15)
- knowing what you are saying (v. 16)
- instruction (v. 19)
- mature thinking (v. 20)
- conviction (v. 24)
- calling to account (v. 24)
- the secrets of the heart disclosed (v. 25)
- falling on the face and worshiping God (v. 25)
- God among you (v. 25)
- psalm (v. 26)
- silence (v. 28)
- learning (v. 31)
- not a God of confusion but of peace (v. 33)

- as in all the churches (v. 33)
- the Lord's commandment (v. 37)
- all things done properly and in an orderly manner (v. 40)

These words and phrases point up central elements in corporate worship (preaching, singing, praying) in common with the people of God in all ages, key motivations and objectives in corporate worship (congregational edification, engagement with God, the by-product of witness to unbelievers), the heart aspects of true worship (consolation, conviction, disclosure, subjection), and concern for form and order (silence, subjection, propriety). But the overwhelming impression made by a review of this service is the cognitive stress of Paul: he wants people to understand what they sing and pray and what others say and preach; he wants instruction, teaching, learning, knowledge, and mature thinking. For those who parody the supposedly overly cerebral corporate worship of the Reformed tradition, there will be utterly no comfort found for them in the description of the charismatic worship of 1 Corinthians 14![20]

Paul regulates the number and order of people allowed to exercise extraordinary gifts vested in them by the Holy Spirit during corporate worship! One cannot conceive of such a restriction on "worship in all of life." Here are his rules:

> If anyone speaks in a tongue, it should be by two or at the most three, and each in turn, and one must interpret; but if there is no interpreter, he must keep silent in the church. (1 Cor. 14:27–28)

20. Robert Webber, for instance, makes this charge frequently. This is typical of the diet: "For centuries the focus of Protestant thought about worship has been on worship as a cerebral act." Robert Webber, "Reaffirming the Arts," *Worship Leader* 8, no. 6 (Nov./Dec. 1999): 10.

Let two or three prophets speak, and let the others pass judgment. But if a revelation is made to another who is seated, the first one must keep silent. For you can all prophesy one by one, so that all may learn and all may be exhorted; and the spirits of prophets are subject to prophets. (14:29–32)

Did you catch that? He said that no more than three shall speak in tongues or prophesy in a given service, and then only one at a time, even if God himself has granted one a prophetic revelation. There is no more astounding example of the sheer investment of dominical plenipotentiary authority in the apostles of the church in all of the holy Scriptures than we find here in this passage. If I could reverently suggest an imaginary dialogue:

"But Paul, I have just received a prophetic revelation of God and I am constrained to disclose it."

"One at a time," says Paul.

"But Paul, God the Holy Spirit has given this word to me."

"I understand—let me repeat, it's one at a time and if three have already spoken, remain silent," replies Paul.

"Paul, how can you? I am a prophet of the Lord!"

"Because, my dear brother, what I speak is the Lord's command for all the churches," says Paul.

Here we have the revelational regulation of corporate worship extending even to activity generated and enabled by the third person of the Trinity. The idea that order, or a concern for it, is inimical to the work of the Spirit and our response to it is dashed against the rocks by this new-covenant passage. The suggestion that applying the rule and order of Scripture will somehow quench the Spirit in corporate worship looks fairly ludicrous in light of this passage. Because God the Spirit who wrote the Lord's command is the same Spirit who enables true worship, there can be no ultimate conflict between form and freedom, between the rules of Scripture and the heartfelt expression of praise, between the precepts of worship and unfettered engagement with God.

Paul puts restrictions on those who may preach the Word in the corporate worship of the churches. He says: "The women are to keep silent in the churches; for they are not permitted to speak, but are to subject themselves, just as the Law also says. If they desire to learn anything, let them ask their own husbands at home; for it is improper for a woman to speak in church" (1 Cor. 14:34–35). Paul grounds this injunction not on some temporary cultural problem in Corinth but in the written Word of God ("just as the Law also says"). There is no more easily observable example of the widespread rejection of the authority of Scripture in the worship of the church than in the ever-growing number of female preachers (however sincere, dedicated, talented, and otherwise orthodox they may be), even in ostensibly evangelical circles. Paul's directive, however, is unmistakable. God's Word alone determines who may or may not preach in public worship.

Paul views his commands as requisite for the corporate worship in all churches, and not simply for Corinth. He says: "If anyone thinks he is a prophet or spiritual, let him recognize that the things which I write to you are the Lord's commandment. But if anyone does not recognize this, he is not recognized" (1 Cor. 14:37–38). This comes in the wake of Paul's declaring his rules on the ordering of tongues, interpretation, prophecy, preaching, and singing, as well as his prohibition of the teaching of women. Why must it be this way? Because, Paul says earlier, "God is not a God of confusion but of peace, as in all the churches of the saints" (14:33). God is not a God of bedlam, and since the same God is God of all his churches the same norms obtain: "All things must be done properly and in an orderly manner"

(14:40). Once again we see that the major thrust of this whole passage is that God cares very much how we worship; he cares not just about our attitudes and motives, but about our actions and order. It is beyond debate that in the new-covenant era God continues to be concerned about how we worship, even though the specifics of the how of worship change from those of the old-covenant ceremonial system.

It is also apparent, even from this abstract of New Testament teaching pertaining to worship (without the benefit of exploring key texts like 1 Cor. 11), that the New Testament has a distinctive category of corporate worship and that it has a special concern about worship that is uniquely and distinguishably corporate. This is important to say because serious voices in the worship debate question whether a distinct category of corporate worship can be found in the new-covenant era. Some suggest that we need to rethink altogether why the church gathers in the first place. For worship? They argue: No, that is not the New Testament answer. The New Testament does not apply the corporate-worship language and terms of the Old Testament to the gathered activity of the local church, but rather to all of life. Therefore, the prime reason we come together is to fellowship, study the Bible, hear preaching, pray together, and the like, but not to worship God—that is what we do in our homes, communities, and vocations.[21] So, in this view, the New Testament fulfillment of Old Testament corporate worship is worship in all of life.

This is a creative approach, to say the least, and it rightly stresses the New Testament's emphasis on worship in all of life

21. For instance, Phillip Jensen and Tony Payne, "Church/Campus Connections," in *Telling the Truth: Evangelizing Postmoderns*, ed. D. A. Carson (Grand Rapids: Eerdmans, 2000), 202-3.

(which is, of course, not without precedent in the Old Testament) and provides enough exegetical grounds and theological critique to prove fatal to any and all prescriptive high church liturgical approaches to worship, but its word-study method does not do justice to the obvious continuities between the elements of Old and New Testament gathered worship (Bible reading, Bible exposition, singing, prayer, and sacraments). No matter what semantic designation is given in the New Testament for the general activity of the gathered people of God when it is engaged in reading, praying, preaching, and singing the Word, it is clear that this constitutes corporate worship and that such a thing does exist even and especially in the new covenant. Only our modern tendencies toward individualism and reticence about distinctions blind us to this fact.

But the Bible does more than show us that there is such a thing as corporate worship and that God cares about how it is done. The Bible testifies, in both New Testament and Old, in its teaching about God and his enduring moral norms, by precept and example, that corporate worship is to be conducted in careful response to divine revelation. And thus we can say that the Bible itself provides us with what the Reformed tradition sometimes labels the regulative principle of worship. Much of what we have already learned substantiates this assertion, but in order to establish this point beyond the shadow of a doubt we will consider in the next chapter, not simply individual passages, but some of the broader theological themes of Scripture that provide the grounds for this distinctive approach to the form and content of biblical corporate worship.

PART TWO

FOUNDATIONS FOR
BIBLICALLY DIRECTED
WORSHIP

The Bible provides us with God's directions for the form and content of Christian worship. When we say that "the acceptable way of worshiping the true God is instituted by himself, and so limited by his own revealed will, that he may not be worshiped according to the imaginations and devices of men, or the suggestions of Satan, under any visible representation, or any other way not prescribed in the holy Scripture,"[1] we anchor that assertion in a number of ways. Our affirmation is grounded not only in the exegesis of specific texts (like Ex. 20:4–6; Deut. 4:15–19; 12:32; Matt. 4:9–10; 15:9; Acts 17:24–25; 1 Cor. 11:23–30; 14:1–40; and Col. 2:16–23) and not only in the transcanonical refrain that God does not desire humanly devised worship. We build also and especially on a set of even broader biblical theological realities: the doctrine of God, the Creator-creature distinction, the idea of revelation, the unchanging character of the moral law, the nature of faith, the doctrine of carefulness, the derivative nature of the church's authority, the doctrine of Christian freedom, the true nature of biblical piety, and the reality of the fallen human nature's tendency to idolatry. Each of these key foundations for the Reformed view of the biblical doctrine of worship is worth consideration. We will explore each one briefly, concluding with a look at the testimony of church history to the Bible's teaching on worship.

1. Westminster Confession of Faith 21.1.

FOUNDATIONAL REALITIES

The Nature of God

God's own nature—who God is—determines the way we should worship him. This is a primary principle of worship in both old and new covenants. In Deuteronomy 4:15–19, the second commandment's prohibition against images in worship is explicitly grounded in Israel's not having seen an image of God, which is, of course, in turn grounded in the nature of God's being. Again, this is precisely what Jesus told the Samaritan woman in John 4:24: "God is spirit, and those who worship Him must worship in spirit and truth." Whatever it means to worship in spirit and truth, Jesus unmistakably bases the requirement of it on the notion that "God is spirit," that is, he grounds it in the nature of God, in theology proper. So, in one sense, our doctrine of worship is an implication of our doctrine of God. This means that the how of new-covenant worship is not ultimately derived from temporary, transitional, positive law or even new-covenant norms, but is based rather upon the character of God himself. As R.C. Sproul often reminds us, the distinctive of the Reformed doctrine of God is that theology proper controls every aspect of our theology, including our worship. Correspondingly, corporate worship as the *locus* of God's prime means of grace is the instrument that God has chosen to grow and edify his church in the knowledge of himself, as well as the vehicle of our special earthly communion with him (Matt. 18). So, the regulative principle is grounded in God's character and not merely in some peculiarity of the Sinai covenant.

The parallel truth to the above point (that God's nature determines the nature of his worship) is that corporate worship informs our understanding of God and therefore must be superintended by him if his self-revelation is to be the prime factor in our knowing him. This is one of the underlying rationales of

Exodus 20:4–6. If you worship God via the usage of images, it changes your view of God. Form impacts content. The means of worship influences the worshipers' apprehension of God. So, Christian corporate worship both requires and shapes our understanding of the Bible's teaching about God. The doctrine of God informs our corporate worship, and, in turn, our corporate worship refines our practical comprehension and embrace of the doctrine of God.

It is true, of course, that worship in all of life impacts our corporate worship. Those who do not "present [their] bodies a living and holy sacrifice" are both unprepared to enter into the fullness of corporate worship as it is envisioned in the Word and are not expressing one of its principal intended ethical effects. In fact, the person in whom there is an experiential dissonance between activity in gathered worship and worship in the rest of life is in danger of creating a parallel but juxtaposed life, the breeding ground of a fatal spiritual hypocrisy. Nevertheless, it is especially in the local church under the means of grace appointed by God for the edification of the church in corporate worship—that is, through the Word (reading, preaching, singing the Bible), prayer (pleading the promises of the Bible, adoring and thanking the God of the Bible, confessing sin, interceding for the saints), and the sacraments (the divinely appointed tangible confirmatory signs of Bible promises)—that we come to know God.

This context provides for both the revelational and relational aspects of Christian discipleship necessary for growth in the knowledge of God. Consequently, the how of worship is vital to our growth in grace and in the knowledge of the one true God because it contributes to our grasp of the one true God. Often we hear, and agree with, the dictum that "we become like what we worship," but the Reformed understanding of worship teaches us that it is also true that "we become like *how* we worship."

The Creator-Creature Distinction

The Bible's inviolable Creator-creature distinction influences the way we worship and makes necessary the regulative principle. The Bible celebrates that distinction from beginning to end. Genesis 1 emphasizes that God made the world and rules over the world and is not a part of or contained within the creation. Over and over we are reminded that he is God and we are not: "Know that the LORD Himself is God; it is He who has made us, and not we ourselves; we are His people" (Ps. 100:3, see also Ezek. 28:2). Repeatedly we are taught his incommunicable attributes and the irreversible discontinuities between his being and ours: "God is not a man, that He should lie, nor a son of man, that He should repent; has He said, and will He not do it? Or has He spoken, and will He not make it good?" (Num. 23:19). Emphatically we are pointed not only to his moral but to his majestic holiness: "I saw the Lord sitting on a throne, lofty and exalted, with the train of His robe filling the temple. Seraphim stood above Him, each having six wings: with two he covered his face, and with two he covered his feet, and with two he flew. And one called out to another and said, 'Holy, Holy, Holy, is the LORD of hosts, The whole earth is full of His glory'" (Isa. 6:1–3). All of these highlight God's transcendence and the inability of our finite minds to fathom him.

So, if worship is going to be in accordance with God's nature, and his nature is transcendent, infinite, and incomprehensible, then how else can we worship other than by the direction of his Word? Once again, our doctrine of God impinges upon our doctrine of worship. Given the distance between Creator and creature (a point of emphasis in Calvin, the Scholastics, Westminster, Van Til, and even Barth!), given the undeniable biblical reality that God's ways and thoughts are as high above ours as the heavens are above the earth (Isa. 55:8–9), what makes us think we can possibly fathom what would please God, apart from his telling us what to do in his Word?[2] The Westminster Assembly stated this argument more than 350 years ago: "The distance between God and the creature is so great that although reasonable creatures do owe obedience unto him as their Creator, yet they could never have any fruition of him as their blessedness and reward but by some voluntary condescension on God's part" (7.1).

The Nature of Revelation and Knowledge

The biblical idea of revelation and knowledge requires revelation-directed worship. Biblical worship inherently entails a response to revelation. As in the covenants, in which God sought out the patriarchs and took initiative in promise and blessing, to which they responded in faith and thanksgiving, so also God takes the initiative in worship. This is necessary now, not only because his nature determines worship and because his nature is infinite, but also because of the blinding impediment of sin: "Although the light of nature, and the works of creation and providence, do so far manifest the goodness, wisdom, and power of God, as to leave men unexcusable; yet are they not sufficient to give that knowledge of God, and of his will, which is necessary unto salvation."[3] It is also necessary for right worship, because of our sin: "Therefore it pleased the Lord, at sundry times, and in divers manners, to reveal himself, and to declare that his will unto his church,"[4] especially regarding the central issue of worship.

---

2. I have been greatly stimulated in my thinking throughout this section by T. David Gordon's "Nine Lines of Argument in Favor of the Regulative Principle of Worship," which originated as class lectures in his ecclesiology courses at Gordon-Conwell Theological Seminary and circulates in various places on the internet. His language can be detected occasionally in mine.

3. Westminster Confession of Faith 1.1, based on Rom. 1:18-20; 1 Cor. 1:21; 2:12-14

4. Westminster Confession of Faith 1.1, based on Heb. 1:1

As revelation is the divine foundation of human knowledge of salvation, so also is revelation the divine foundation of our worship of God, which is itself, when properly understood, a response to revelation. And if worship is to be a right response to revelation, then it must be revelationally directed. Hence, we see the dialogical aspect in worship of God's call and our response. God takes initiative in worship through revelation, promise, and blessing. His people respond in worship through hearing and believing and through praise, adoration, confession, and thanksgiving. This divine, covenantal pattern is reflected in the true worship of every biblical age, whatever the peculiar distinctives, and yields the irreducible core of reading, preaching (God's initiative in revelation), singing, and praying (our response to revelation) in accordance with divine revelation. R. P. Martin puts it this way: "The distinctive genius of corporate worship is the two-beat rhythm of revelation and response. God speaks; we answer. God acts; we accept and give. God gives; we receive. As a corollary to this picture, worship implies a code word for man's offering to God: *sacrifice*. The worshiper is not a passive, motionless recipient, but an active participant, called upon to 'make an offering.'"[5]

The Second Commandment

The enduring moral norm of the second commandment necessitates that true worship conform to the regulative principle. We have already seen in our study of the second commandment that it forbids not only the making of idols, not only the use of images in the worship of the one true God, not only the introduction of things forbidden into the worship of God, but also of anything not commanded or warranted. The abiding

5. R. P. Martin, *The Worship of God: Some Theological, Pastoral, and Practical Reflections* (Grand Rapids: Eerdmans, 1982), 6.

validity of this command is seen in its placement in the moral, not the ceremonial law; in its reflection of the character of God and not of changing moral norms; in the constant repetition of its core principle throughout Scripture; and in Paul's characterization of obedience to it as the essence of Christianity ("you turned to God from idols to serve a living and true God"; 1 Thess. 1:9). This is, by the way, why Robert Dabney calls the New Testament "a Book intended to subvert idolatry."[6]

Indeed, the New Testament, precisely because of the abiding validity of the second commandment as an unchanging moral norm, even extends the Old Testament critique of idolatry further. Since there is a double essence to the idolatry prohibited in the second command (worshiping something other than the one true God or worshiping the one true God in a way he has not commanded), we must rely on the regulative principle to assist us in avoiding idolatrous worship. Thus the *elements* of worship must be instituted by God himself, the *forms* in which those elements are performed must not be inimical to the nature or content of the element or draw attention away from the substance and goal of worship, and the *circumstances* of worship must never overshadow or detract from the elements, but rather discreetly foster the work of the means of grace.

The Nature of Faith

Related to the biblical teaching regarding revelation and knowledge is another important building block of the Reformed approach to worship. It is called "the argument from faith" (and John Owen, for instance, states it convincingly). Since faith is essential to true worship, the conditions of worship must accord with the exercise of true faith. Faith is, in essence, a believing

---

6. Robert L. Dabney, *Lectures in Systematic Theology* (Grand Rapids: Baker, 1985), 183.

response to God's revelation, especially his revelation of cove- .
nant and promise. As the Westminster Confession says, by faith
"a Christian believes to be true whatsoever is revealed in the
word, for the authority of God himself speaking therein; and
acts differently upon that which each particular passage thereof
contains; yielding obedience to the commands, trembling at the
threatenings, and embracing the promises of God for this life,
and that which is to come" (14.2). Where God has not revealed
himself, there can be no faithful response to his revelation, by
virtue of the very nature of faith. Since "without faith it is impossible to please [God]" (Heb. 11:6) and since "whatever is not
from faith is sin" (Rom. 14:23), God cannot be pleased by worship that is not an obedient response to his revelation, because it
is by definition "un-faith-full" worship. Hence, once again we see
that worship must be positively based upon the Word of God.

The Doctrine of Carefulness

The Bible makes it exceedingly clear that we ought to be
careful in worship. Our God is a consuming fire and not to be
trifled with. The severity of the punishments inflicted upon
those who from time to time offered to God, apparently in good
faith, unprescribed worship catches our attention: the stories of
Nadab and Abihu and their "strange fire" (Lev. 10:1–2) and of
Uzzah and David and the ark (2 Sam. 6).

But biblical doctrine of carefulness in worship is built on an
even broader foundation than these breathtaking warning passages. It is supported by at least the following scriptural truths:

- We were created to worship God, and hence the fulfillment of our very purpose behooves us to take care in
  how we worship.
- Corporate worship dictates the quality of our worship
  in all of life and compels our carefulness.

- That God himself is seeking worshipers who will worship him in spirit and in truth constrains all who would be those worshipers to acquaint themselves with care as to just how one goes about worshiping in spirit and truth.
- God is dangerous to those who are careless in worship, however sincere.

Thus the Reformed tradition has always understood that, especially in worship, the road to destruction is paved with good intentions. Intentions are not enough; we must submit ourselves to the authority of the Word, be mindful to learn and obey the Word, and neglect no part of the Word. The way of carefulness is the way of the Word and so corroborates the regulative principle.

The Church's Derivative Authority

The Bible's teaching on the derivative nature of the church's authority limits its discretionary powers in worship and enjoins its observance of the regulative principle. Jesus is the sole King of and lawmaker for the church (Matt. 28:18–20). All the authority of the church derives from him. The ordinary officers of the church, as gifts of Christ for its upbuilding (Eph. 4:11–13), have no authority to instate their own laws and norms; their job is to administer his rule and law, revealed in the Word. This is one reason that Presbyterians refer to their church councils and assemblies as "courts" (not legislatures). Their job is to administer the king's law, not to make it. Thus all church power is "ministerial and declarative." That is, it serves the Word and declares the will of the King of the church.

James Bannerman makes this argument in *The Church of Christ*: "The Church is an institution; instituted by the positive command of the risen Christ, and authorized by Him to require obedience to His commands and participation in His ordinances. The Church is given no authority to require obedience to its own commands, and is given no authority to require participation in ordinances of its own making."[7] If this is the case, then it is not surprising that Christ has not left the church with discretionary authority in the matter of the substance and elements of worship. It is the church's business simply to administer his rule for worship, as set forth in the Word. So, this regulative principle of church government lies behind and necessitates the regulative principle of worship.

The Doctrine of Christian Freedom

The biblical doctrine of Christian freedom is vital to our doctrine of worship and can be protected only by the regulative principle. The Westminster Confession makes the bold declaration that "God alone is Lord of the conscience, and has left it free from the doctrines and commandments of men which are in any thing contrary to his word, or beside it in matters of faith or worship. So that to believe such doctrines, or to obey such commands out of conscience, is to betray true liberty of conscience; and the requiring of an implicit faith, and an absolute and blind obedience, is to destroy liberty of conscience, and reason also" (20.2). This manifesto of Christian freedom is based on Pauline principles found in Romans 14:1–4, Galatians 4:8–11, and Colossians 2:16–23.

The regulative principle is designed to secure the believer's freedom from the dominion of human opinion in worship. But some people view the regulative principle as legalistic and constraining. They rightly note that it forbids a variety of activities and restrains others; but this is simply to say that it helps enforce biblical norms that are, upon reflection, freeing!

7. Quoted in Gordon, "Nine Lines of Argument."

Freedom from human opinions can be found only in the rule of God's good and gracious and wise law. If humans can dictate how we may worship, apart from the Word or in addition to the Word, then we are captive to their command. The only way we can really experience one of the key blessings of Christian freedom in the context of corporate worship—freedom from human doctrines and commandments—is if corporate worship is directed only according to the Word of God, and that means following the regulative principle. Furthermore "God requires us to worship Him only as He has revealed. Therefore, to require a person, in corporate worship, to do something that God has not required, forces the person to sin against his/her conscience, by making them do what they do not believe God has called them to do."[8]

The Nature of True Piety

God repeatedly expresses his pleasure with and delight in those who do exactly what he says. In Isaiah 66:1–4, true religion ("the life of God in the soul of man") is characterized by one "who is humble and contrite of spirit, and who trembles at My word" in contrast to these who choose their own way. Deuteronomy 12:29–32 explicitly warns against establishing worship practices based upon prevailing cultural norms; true godliness is manifested in those who obey God's dictum: "Whatever I command you, you shall be careful to do; you shall not add to nor take away from it." In the Saul stories a dominant theme is that "to obey is better than sacrifice" (1 Sam. 15:3–22), a thought that puts a premium on strict obedience to God's Word in corporate worship. True piety manifests itself in humble obedience to God's Word in our expression of worship and thus urges us to worship that is wholly in accord with Scripture.

8. Quoted in Gordon, "Nine Lines of Argument."

Our Tendency to Idolatry

The biblical teaching on our fallen human tendency to idolatry affects our approach to the worship of God and moves us to embrace the regulative principle. Calvin called our minds "perpetual idol factories." Experience confirms his less-than-flattering estimation. Indeed, idolatry, not theoretical atheism, is the basic problem of the human heart. Luther said that "we are inclined to it by nature; and coming to us by inheritance, it seems pleasant." Humanity, having been created in God's image, and with a sense of deity indelibly written on its heart, is inescapably religious. However, since the fall, our tendency is to attempt to create God in our own image and thus worship ourselves rather than the one in whose image we were made. This is precisely Paul's argument in Romans 1:19–25:

> That which is known about God is evident within them; for God made it evident to them. For since the creation of the world His invisible attributes, His eternal power and divine nature, have been clearly seen, being understood through what has been made, so that they are without excuse. For even though they knew God, they did not honor Him as God or give thanks, but they became futile in their speculations, and their foolish heart was darkened. Professing to be wise, they became fools, and exchanged the glory of the incorruptible God for an image in the form of corruptible man and of birds and four-footed animals and crawling creatures.
>
> Therefore God gave them over in the lusts of their hearts to impurity, so that their bodies would be dishonored among them. For they exchanged the truth of God for a lie, and worshiped and served the creature rather than the Creator.

This indictment charges that though God's general revelation of himself is evident in and to the natural person, as well as in the larger creation, thus leaving us without defense against God's charges of rebellion, nevertheless this knowledge does not lead to worship and thanksgiving but to idolatry. It is part of Paul's accusation against the whole of humanity—Jew and Gentile. This is why even John Wesley could say that in his natural state, every man born into the world is a rank idolater.

Now, if this is true of us apart from God's saving grace, then a proper understanding of the ongoing depravity of the Christian life, the reality of indwelling sin, a knowledge of how master-sins work, an appreciation of the gradual and partial work of progressive sanctification, and an appropriate humility and self-knowledge ought to move us to avoid human invention and to be careful of human creativity in worship. We are all recovering idolaters. Extreme caution is needed when it comes to how we worship. In the final analysis, the world is divided into iconoclasts and iconodules. You must decide on which side you will stand.

The Testimony of Church History

The testimony (both positive and negative) of church history to the Bible's teaching on worship educates our worship and commends to us worship according to Scripture. Church history does not supply a normative authority for Christian worship, but it does supply a didactic authority that we would be foolish to ignore. As Hughes Old says: "In the last analysis we are not as much concerned about what the tradition tells us about worship as we are concerned with what tradition tells us about what Scripture has to say about worship."[9] What does Christian history teach us? Several things:

9. Hughes Oliphant Old, *Worship That Is Reformed according to Scripture* (Atlanta: John Knox, 1984), 170–71.

- Simple but powerful biblical worship always characterizes the worship of the church in its best ages. The testimony of the healthiest Christianity is to Bible-filled, Bible-directed worship, worship in which the Scriptures are read, preached, sung, and prayed and the sacraments, as visible words, are administered in accordance with the word written—this is precisely what the regulative principle seeks to foster in the church today.

- There is every evidence in both biblical and postbiblical church history that declension in corporate worship is tied to declension in religion.

- Following on this, church history shows that even Christians, left to their own devices, inevitably produce worship that is unbiblical and impious. The Reformation was a gigantic protest against exactly this.

- History is not normative, but it helps us to understand Scripture, and it gives us perspective on the peculiar tendencies and temptations of our own age. The sweep of Christian history provides an opportunity to sit at the feet of the *sanctorum communio* and learn wisdom, to have our priorities weighed and measured and our practices compared and contrasted, in ways that they could not be otherwise. Both the accomplishments and the mistakes of the past bring didactic and diagnostic help to us as we attempt to faithfully worship according to the Scripture in our own time and cultural situation.

- Finally, the best of Christian history instructs and inspires us for our worship today. Not that our worship can ever be a mere photocopy of the past; but an appreciation of the devotional treasures of the ages bequeathed to us in the legacy of the historic worship of the church helps us resist the rampant chronological snobbery of our own age.

KNOWING THAT, WHAT, WHOM, WHEN, WHERE, WHY, AND HOW

The foundational realities described above are connected and compounding and serve to corroborate the legitimacy and importance of the regulative principle—the axiom that we ought to worship God in accordance with the positive warrant of Scripture. This axiom applied, in turn, helps us with the whole scope of worship. Thus historic Reformed worship appreciates God's concern for the that, what, whom, when, where, why, and how of corporate worship.

It is important *that* we worship corporately, for God made us for his worship and for community with other worshipers. Worship is the one thing he "seeks" (John 4:23).

What corporate worship is matters to God too. It is not evangelism, nor is it even mutually edifying fellowship. It is a family meeting with God; it is the covenant community engaging with God, gathering with his people to seek the face of God, to glorify and enjoy him, to hear his Word, to revel in the glory of union and communion with him, to respond to his Word, to render praise back to him, to give unto him the glory due his name. John Piper puts it this way:

> The authenticating, inner essence of worship is being satisfied with Christ, prizing Christ, cherishing Christ, treasuring Christ . . . . [This] is tremendously relevant for understanding what worship services should be about. They are about "going hard after God."
>
> When we say that what we do on Sunday mornings is to "go hard after God," what we mean is that we are going hard after satisfaction in God, and going hard after God as our prize, and going hard after God as our treasure, our soul-food, our heart-delight, our spirit's pleasure. Or to put Christ in His

71

rightful place—it means that we are going hard after all that God is for us in Jesus Christ, crucified and risen.[10]

Worship is both active and passive: we come to bless and to receive God's blessing (Ps. 134). Christian corporate worship is Father-focused, Christ-centered, and Spirit-enabled (Eph. 1:3–14) and "offered up in the context of the body of believers, who strive to align all the forms of their devout ascription of all worth to God with the panoply of new covenant mandates and examples that bring to fulfillment the glories of antecedent revelation and anticipated the consummation."[11]

The *whom* of worship is, of course, central to true worship (John 4:22, 24). It is what the first commandment is all about. We aim to worship the God of the Bible, God as he reveals himself, for we cannot worship him as we ought unless we know him as he is—and we cannot know him as he is except insofar as he has revealed himself to us in his Word. There is a god we want and the God who is, and the two are not the same.[12] The only way to be sure that we have the whom of worship right is to worship according to God's written self-revelation.

The *when* of corporate worship remains important in the new-covenant era. In the days of the old covenant, worship was to be rendered on the seventh day because of God's creational rest and on the various feast days that foreshadowed new-covenant realities. Now, in the end of the ages, corporate

10. John Piper, *Brothers, We Are Not Professionals: A Plea to Pastors for Radical Ministry* (Nashville: Broadman & Holman, 2002), 236.

11. D. A. Carson, "Worship under the Word," in *Worship by the Book*, ed. D. A. Carson (Grand Rapids: Zondervan, 2002), 26.

12. I borrow from and pattern this language after the powerful observation of Pat Morley: *"There is a God we want, and there is a God who is—and they are not the same God. The turning point of our lives is when we stop seeking the God we want and start seeking the God who is." The Rest of Your Life* (Nashville: Nelson, 1992), 120 (emphasis original).

worship is to be done on the first day of the week, the Lord's Day. Even for those who do not embrace the Reformed view of the Christian Sabbath, four tremendous realities establish the importance of Lord's Day corporate worship:

- the resurrection of Christ, which is foundational to the recreative work of Christ in making a people for himself (Mark 16:1–8; cf. v. 9; 2 Cor. 5:14–17; Gal. 6:15–16; Col. 1:15–22);
- the eternal rest foreshadowed in the Lord's Day (Heb. 4:9);
- the Lord's Day language and observance of the New Testament church (Rev. 1:10; cf. Matt. 28:1; Luke 24:1; John 20:1,19–23; Acts 20:7; 1 Cor. 16:2); and
- the New Testament command to the saints to gather, Christ's promise of presence with us when we do, the faithful example of the gathering of New Testament Christians, and Jesus's express command that we disciple new converts in the context of the local church (Heb. 10:24–25; Matt. 18:20; 28:18–20; Acts 1:4).

The *where* of new-covenant worship is important too, though it has also changed from the old-covenant era. Whereas once the answer to where was "the tabernacle" or "the temple" or "Jerusalem," the answer now is "wherever the Lord's house (i.e., his people) is gathered." Jesus stresses this to the Samaritan woman (John 4:21) and to his disciples in addressing congregational discipline (Matt. 18:20)—surely a solemn component of the life of the gathered church. The place of new-covenant worship is no longer inextricably tied to a geographical location and a physical structure but to a gathered people. This is why in the old Scottish tradition, as the people gathered to enter a church building, it would be said that "the kirk goes in" rather than, as we often say, "we are going to church." The new covenant locus of the special presence of God with the church militant is in the gathered body, wherever it might be—whether the catacombs or a storefront or beautiful colonial church building.

The *why* of corporate worship is vital to God as well, and there is more than one right biblical answer. Surely at the top of the list is "for his own glory" (1 Cor. 10:31; Ps. 29:1–2). There is no higher answer to "why do we worship?" than because the glory of God is more important than anything else in all creation. The chief end of the church is to glorify and enjoy God together forever, because the chief thing in all the world is God's glory (Phil. 2:9–11). John Piper communicates this as effectively as anyone in our generation. There are other answers as well: because God said to worship, because God created us to worship, because God saved us to worship, because it is our natural duty as creatures and joyful duty as Christians to worship, because our worship is a response of gratitude for saving grace, because those with new hearts long to hear his Word and express their devotion, because God wants to bless us with himself, because God has chosen us for his own inheritance and seeks to commune with us in his ordinances, and more.

The *how* of corporate worship is the business of the second commandment, but as we have seen, it is a central concern for the New Testament church as well (John 4; 1 Cor. 11, 14; Col. 2). This is where the regulative principle is manifest most clearly. It is concerned to assure that corporate worship in all its aspects—standard, dynamic, motivation, and goal—is biblical. For the standard to be biblical means that the substance and elements and corporateness of worship are positively in accord with Scripture. For the dynamic to be biblical means that worship is Spirit-gathered, Spirit-dependent, Spirit-engendered, and Spirit-empowered, in accordance with the teaching of

Scripture. For the motivation to be biblical means that worship is simultaneously a communal response of gratitude for grace, an expression of passion for God, the fulfillment of what we were made and redeemed for, a joyful engagement in a delightful obedience, and a corporate Christ-provided encounter with the triune God, again in accord with the Bible's teaching. For the goal to biblical means that all true corporate worship aims for and is an expression of God's own glory and contemplates the consummation of the eternal covenant in the church triumphant's everlasting union and communion with God.

The regulative principle aims to aid the church in ensuring that the elements of worship are unequivocally and positively grounded in Scripture and that the forms and circumstances of worship are in accord with Scripture. The Reformed tradition has not been concerned with forms and circumstances so much for their own sake as much as for the sake of the elements and substance of worship and for the sake of the object and aim of worship.

The Reformers also understood two things often lost on moderns. First, they understood that the liturgy, media, instruments, and vehicles of worship are never neutral, and so exceeding care must be given to the "law of unintended consequences." Often the medium overwhelms and changes the message. Second, they knew that the how of worship exists for the what, whom, and why of worship. The purpose of the elements and forms and circumstances of corporate worship is to assure that you are actually doing worship as defined by the God of Scripture, that you are worshiping the God of Scripture, and that your aim in worshiping him is the aim set forth in Scripture. So the Reformers cared about the how of worship not because they thought liturgy was mystical or sacramental, but precisely so that the liturgy could get out of the way of the gathered church's communion with the living God. Its function was not to draw attention to itself but to aid the soul's communion with God in the gathered company of the saints by serving to convey the Word of God to and from God, from and to his people.

This is why the great Baptist preacher Geoffrey Thomas has said that in true worship men have little thought of the means of worship because their thoughts are on God; true worship is characterized by self-effacement without self-consciousness. That is, in biblical worship we so focus upon God himself and are so intent to acknowledge his inherent and unique worthiness that we are transfixed by him, and thus worship is not about what we want or like (nor do his appointed means divert our eyes from him), but rather it is about meeting with God and delighting in his delights. Praise decentralizes self.

We should also note another thing about the Reformers' approach to worship. They did not have the same interest in cultural accommodation as many modern evangelical worship theorists do. They were against culture-derived worship and were more concerned to implement principles of Scripture in their specific cultures (and even to emulate the best of the Bible-inspired cultures of Scripture) than they were to reclaim current cultural forms for Christian use. This is precisely one of the areas productive of the greatest controversy in our own age.

THE FORM AND CONTENT OF WORSHIP

So far we have outlined a case for the historic Reformed approach to worship, often called the regulative principle. The regulative principle helps to ensure that our corporate worship is Bible-filled and Bible-directed, that the substance and structure are biblical, that the content and order are biblical. To put it slightly differently, Reformed corporate worship is by the book in two ways: both its marrow and means are supplied by the book.

What then does a worship service look like that is done

according to the regulative principle? The Westminster Confession outlines the components this way: "The reading of the Scriptures with godly fear; the sound preaching; and conscionable hearing of the word, in obedience unto God with understanding, faith, and reverence; singing of psalms[13] with grace in the heart; as, also, the due administration and worthy receiving of the sacraments instituted by Christ; are all parts of the ordinary religious worship of God: beside religious oaths, vows, solemn fastings, and thanksgivings upon special occasions; which are, in their several times and seasons, to be used in an holy and religious manner" (21.5).

What is striking about the Reformed approach to worship is that it requires the substance of corporate worship to be suffused with Scripture and scriptural theology. An apt motto for those who embrace the regulative principle then might be, "Read the Bible, preach the Bible, pray the Bible, sing the Bible, and see the Bible."

Read the Bible

We are to read the Bible in public worship. Paul told Timothy to "give attention to the public reading of Scripture" (1 Tim. 4:13), and so a worship service influenced by the regulative principle will contain a substantial reading of Scripture (and not just from the sermon text). The public reading of the Bible has been at the heart of the worship of God since Old Testament times. In the reading of God's Word, he speaks most directly to his people. It is one of the sad indictments of evangelical worship today that it has so little Scripture in it. By contrast, the Westminster Assembly's Directory for the Public Worship of God commends the reading of whole chapters!

13. There are good reasons to believe that the Westminster Assembly did not intend by this term to restrict the sung praise of the congregation to the

Preach the Bible

We are to preach the Bible. Preaching is God's prime appointed instrument to build up his church. As Paul says, "Faith comes from hearing" (Rom. 10:14, 17). Faithful biblical preaching is to explain and apply Scripture to the gathered company, believer and unbeliever alike. James Durham puts it this way: "This is the great design of all preaching, to bring them within the covenant who are without, and to make those who are within the covenant to walk suitably to it. And as these are never separated on the Lord's side, so should they never be separated on our side."[14] This means expository and evangelistic preaching, squarely based in the text of the Word of God. This is why our favorite Anglican bishop, J. C. Ryle, can say:

> I charge my readers to remember this. Stand fast on old principles. Do not forsake the old paths. Let nothing tempt you to believe that multiplication of forms and ceremonies, constant reading of liturgical services, or frequent communions, will ever do so much good to souls as the powerful, fiery, fervent preaching of God's Word. Daily services without sermons may gratify and edify a few handfuls of believers, but they will never reach, draw, attract, or arrest the great mass of mankind. If men want to do good to the multitude, if they want to reach their hearts and consciences, they must walk in the steps of Wycliffe, Latimer, Luther, Chrysostom, and St. Paul. They must attack them through their ears; they must blow the trumpet of the everlasting Gospel loud and long; they must preach the Word.[15]

Old Testament Psalter.

14. James Durham, *The Blessed Death of Those Who Die in the Lord* (repr., Morgan, PA: Soli Deo Gloria, 2003).

15. J. C. Ryle, *Light from Old Times* (London: Chas. J. Thynne & Jarves, 1924), 7-8.

People who hold to the regulative principle will have a high view of preaching and little time for the personality-driven, theologically void, superficially practical monologues that pass for preaching today. "From the very beginning the sermon was supposed to be an explanation of the Scripture reading," says Old; it "is not just a lecture on some religious subject, it is rather an explanation of a passage of Scripture."[16] "Preach the word," Paul tells Timothy (2 Tim. 4:2). "Expository, sequential, verse by verse, book by book, preaching through the whole Bible, the 'whole council of God' (Acts 20:27), was the practice of many of the church fathers (e.g., Chrysostom, Augustine), all the Reformers and the best of their heirs ever since. The preached word is the central feature of Reformed worship."[17]

Pray the Bible

We are to pray the Bible. We must restore the pastoral prayer to its former place of dignity. Our prayers ought to be permeated with the language and thought of Scripture. Perhaps the single most obvious departure from the regulative principle in the Reformed churches of today is precisely this absence of substantive prayer. And yet the Father's house "is a house of prayer," said Jesus (Matt. 21:13). Terry Johnson makes the case thusly:

> The pulpit prayers of Reformed churches should be rich in Biblical and theological content. Do we not learn the language of Christian devotion from the Bible? Do we not learn the language of confession and penitence from the Bible? Do we

16. Old, *Worship*, 59-60. See also idem, *The Reading and Preaching of the Scriptures in the Worship of the Christian Church* (Grand Rapids: Eerdmans, 1998), esp. vols. 1-2.

17. Terry Johnson, *Reformed Worship: Worship That Is according to Scripture* (Greenville, SC: Reformed Academic Press, 2000), 35.

not learn the promises of God to believe and claim in prayer from the Bible? Don't we learn the will of God, the commands of God, and the desires of God for His people, for which we are to plead in prayer, from the Bible? Since these things are so, public prayers should repeat and echo the language of the Bible throughout. This was once widely understood. Matthew Henry and Isaac Watts produced prayer manuals that trained Protestant pastors for generations to pray in the language of Scripture, and are still used today. Hughes Old has produced a similar work in recent years.[18]

The call here is not for written and read prayer, but studied free prayer. Ministers ought to spend time plundering the language of Scripture in preparation for leading in public worship.

Sing the Bible

We are to sing the Bible (Ps. 98:1; Neh. 12:27,46; Matt. 26:30; Acts 16:25; Eph. 5:19; Col. 3:16; Rev. 5:9). This does not mean that we can sing only psalms or sing only the language of Scripture, though this tremendous doxological resource of the church should not be overlooked. What we mean by "sing the Bible" is that our singing ought to be biblical, shot through with the language, categories, and theology of the Bible. It ought to reflect the themes and proportion of the Bible, as well as its substance and weightiness. Johnson provides this counsel:

> Our songs should be rich with Biblical and theological content. The current divisions over music are at the heart of our

18. Johnson, 36-37. The books referred to are Matthew Henry, *Method for Prayer*, ed. J. Ligon Duncan III (Greenville, SC: Reformed Academic Press, 1994); Isaac Watts, *A Guide to Prayer* (repr., Edinburgh: Banner of Truth, 2001); and Hughes Oliphant Old, *Leading in Prayer* (Grand Rapids: Eerdmans, 1995).

worship wars. Yet some principles should be easy enough to identify. First, what does a Christian worship song look like? Answer, it looks like a Psalm. Reformed Protestants have sometimes exclusively sung Psalms. But even if that is not one's conviction, one should still acknowledge that the Psalms themselves should be sung and that the Psalms provide the model for Christian hymnody. If the songs we sing in worship look like Psalms, they will develop themes over many lines with minimal repetition. They will be rich in theological and experiential content. They will tell us much about God, man, sin, salvation, and the Christian life. They will express the whole range of human experience and emotion. Second, what does a Christian worship song *sound* like? Many are quick to point out that God has not given us a book of tunes. No, but He has given us a book of lyrics (the Psalms) and their form will do much to determine the kinds of tunes that will be used. Put simply, the tunes will be suited to the words. They will be sophisticated enough to carry substantial content over several lines and stanzas. They will use minimal repetition. They will be appropriate to the emotional mood of the Psalm or Bible-based Christian hymn. Sing the Bible.[19]

See the Bible

We are to see the Bible. We say "see" the Bible because God's sacraments are "visible words" (Augustine's phrase). The sacraments (baptism and the Lord's Supper) are the only two commanded dramas of Christian worship (Matt. 28:19; Acts 2:38–39; Col. 2:11–12; Luke 22:14–20; 1 Cor. 11:23–26). In them we see the promise of God. But we could also say that in the sacraments we see, smell, touch, and taste the Word. In the other means of grace, God addresses our mind and conscience

19. Johnson, 36-37.

through the hearing. In the sacraments, he uniquely addresses our mind and conscience through the other senses. In, through, and to the senses, God's promise is made tangible.

A sacrament is a covenant sign and seal, which means that it reminds us and assures us of a promise. That is, it points to and confirms a gracious promise of God to his people. Another way of saying it is that a sacrament is an action designed by God to sign and seal a covenantal reality, accomplished by the power and grace of God, the significance of which is communicated by the Word of God and the reality of which is received or entered into by faith. Hence, the weakness, the frailty of human faith welcomes this gracious act of reassurance. And so these visible symbols of gospel truths are to be done as part of our corporate worship. They will be occasional, no matter how frequent, and so we are reminded that they are not essential to every service. This is not to denigrate them in the least. After all, they are by nature supplemental to and confirmatory of the promises held out in the Word, and the grace conveyed in them is the same grace held out via the means of preaching.

There it is. There in a nutshell is the Reformed program for worship. It is simple, biblical, transferable, flexible, and reverent.

Simple

Reformed worship is simple in that it requires no elaborate ritual, no prescribed book of common prayer, but is merely based on the unadorned and unpretentious principles and order found in the Bible, by precept and example, which supply the substance of new-covenant worship. There is, of course, a small but intelligent and literate movement advocating formal liturgical renewal in Reformed evangelicalism. Usually emphasizing the contributions of the early church and the early Reformed liturgies of Strasbourg and Geneva and unwittingly adopting a late-nineteenth-century Scoto-Catholic interpretation of their significance, this movement, open to a more Lutheran view of the sacraments (via the Mercersburg theology) and generally scathing in its estimation of the Westminster Directory and Puritan worship, is working to "liturgicalize" Reformed and evangelical corporate worship.[20] This group propounds what Old calls "Liturgical Romanticism"—the view that, if we could just get back to Bucer's liturgy all would be put right in the church today! This reform effort seems to have captured the imagination of many fine young conservative Reformed ordinands and shares a kinship with "the great tradition" movement evident in broader evangelicalism. This is not our call however. Our call is to something both simpler and more profound. We are not harkening the church to fixed forms from the past, however elegant or even consonant with Reformed worship they may be. We are, instead, calling the church to the Bible—to its simple principles and patterns.

Biblical

We have argued this case over and over and so we shall not repeat or even summarize it here. We will, however, note two things. First, while many present-day worship theorists spend much time seeking to adapt the forms of corporate worship, and especially musical forms, to cultural currencies and see such cultural adaptation as key to reaching the culture, the Reformers were not nearly so interested in that as they were in being biblical. Second, there is a recent common criticism of the kind of worship promoted by the regulative principle that goes like this: Much of what is called historic Reformed worship is derived from northern European culture and binds the church too closely to a past culture.

---

20. A representative example of this tendency is found in Jeffrey J. Meyers, *The Lord's Service* (St. Louis: Providence Presbyterian Church, 1999).

To the second point, what can be said in reply? Is what is called historic Reformed Protestant worship really just an imposition of north European culture on the practice of church? No. Do the principles and elements of historic Protestant worship derive from north European culture? The emphatic answer is no! They are biblically derived, though perhaps more fully implemented in the Reformation and post-Reformation Protestant tradition than anywhere else, and are manifest in churches today on every continent. The argument that historic Protestant worship is north European in essence is no more persuasive than the now-popular assertion that the doctrine of justification by grace alone through faith alone is sixteenth-century European in origin, or the tired old canard than nineteenth-century Americans at Princeton invented the doctrine of biblical inerrancy. It is ironic that some of the very people who make this dismissive assertion are themselves working hard to accommodate Christian worship to a tiny sub-culture. The historic worship norms reclaimed in Europe five centuries ago are not European in origin. They are Jewish! That is not to say that European culture (if we can even speak of such a thing in that time) made no impingement upon what we now identify as "historic worship," but that the Reformers and their successors were not as interested in accommodating their culture (or redeeming it through the forms of worship) as they were in having their worship according to the Word of God.

Transferable

Reformed worship has worked and is working in every situation and culture where there is a historic Protestant church committed to scriptural principles of worship. It is also more culturally transportable for the work of missions than the more elaborate high church forms or the more electronic and entertainment-oriented forms of contemporary worship.

It is easy to provide examples of how this principle is applied globally. You can find it in the following kinds of diverse settings:

Alonzo Ramirez's little congregation in Cajamarca, Peru, up in the Peruvian Andes, gathers in a building they made with their own hands. Sometimes they sing straight out of the text of the Psalms in their Spanish Bibles, sometimes they use Peruvian tunes, sometimes American and British tunes. Here in a nominally Roman Catholic, economically impoverished setting, historic Reformed worship is gathering a congregation.

It is evident in the famous Tenth Presbyterian Church in Philadelphia, where over a thousand gather on a Sunday morning in an enormous nineteenth-century building with architectural allusions to an ancient church in Ravenna, to engage in historic, Reformed, Protestant worship—majestic, simple, and reverent praise of God, using a set order that has been in place since who knows when, with lengthy Scripture readings, traditional hymns, and weighty expository preaching by the able Phil Ryken.

Or go across town to West Philadelphia and visit Lance Lewis at Christ Liberation Fellowship, and you will find a faithful African American pastor, deliberately committed to historic Reformed worship.

You will also see it in any of the many congregations planted by Khen Tombing in India. In the simplest of structures, often in dangerous conditions, people wracked by poverty and terrorism gather every Lord's Day to hear the doctrines of grace proclaimed. Their worship? Read the Bible, preach the Bible, sing the Bible, and pray the Bible. True there are variations in custom and order, but the worship is recognizable, and Khen deliberately follows in the expository tradition of the great Robert G. Rayburn, feeding his people on the meat of the Word.

It is displayed in St. Peter's Free Church in Dundee, Scotland, where David Robertson now ministers. Once the pulpit of Robert Murray M'Cheyne, this venerable old building houses a young, growing, postmodern, psalm-singing congregation that features people from the widest conceivable cultural backgrounds. A dozen or so languages can be heard on their grounds, and they are reaching out to inner-city Dundee and fostering a church-planting movement across Scotland. Their worship is, of course, read the Bible, preach the Bible, sing the Bible, and pray the Bible.

You will find it in the Los Olivos congregation in the slums of Lima, where the faithful William Castro labors. Street children abound, poverty is rife, and this faithful local church is reading, preaching, praying, and singing the Bible. The new Peruvian psalter, it should be said, features tunes from Peru, America, Scotland, Wales, England, France, Germany, Switzerland, Italy, Egypt, and medieval Jewish origins.

Then there is Capitol Hill Baptist Church in Washington, DC, where Cambridge-educated Mark Dever gathers a congregation. Some of their musical forms might be identified as contemporary, but they are substantive, challenging, and reverent, and their service order changes weekly, by pastoral conviction. The sermon is usually an hour or more, and how would I characterize their worship? Read the Bible, preach the Bible, sing the Bible, and pray the Bible.

Go across the Atlantic to Grove Chapel, Camberwell, in London, England, where Mark Johnston faithfully proclaims the Word. What do you find there? Historic, simple, reverent, Reformed, Protestant worship.

Move south, deep into sub-Saharan Africa into the cool green of Malawi. What do Augustine Mfune's congregations of thousands do as they gather on Sunday mornings? They read, hear preached, sing, and pray the Bible.

Then there is St. Helen Bishopsgate, back in London (where Dick Lucas ministered), and I have not spoken of the Independent Presbyterian Church in Savannah, with its Genevaninspired order of service, or Rowland Ward's congregation (Knox Presbyterian Church of Eastern Australia) in Melbourne, Australia, or Reformed churches I know of in Japan and Israel. Do not let anyone tell you that historic Reformed worship will not transfer or that it cannot work outside of Anglo-American culture or in the context of a postmodern generation.

Flexible

Reformed worship does not produce a cookie-cutter pattern. Following the Westminster Directory of Public Worship's guidelines does not eliminate diversity or different cultural expressions in the forms and circumstances of corporate worship (though it does mean that these are emphatically not the "first things" of the how of worship). Consider again the churches mentioned just above, representing Baptist, Presbyterian, Congregational, and low-church Anglican traditions, on six continents, first world and two-thirds world, ministering to every conceivable class of society—they are following in the train of historic Reformed Protestant worship. Their respective liturgies have strengths and weaknesses; the musical forms vary, with some using more contemporary material, others less; there are noticeable differences in the emphases of their worship orders and considerable diversity among them, but in all of them one would find it hard to forget that the Christian church has been worshiping this way for twenty centuries (and that is far more than can be said in many North American and European evangelical churches today). Worship with them and you will find no triteness or trendiness, no "more relevant than thou" antics, just meat and potatoes—simple, spiritual, passionate, biblical, reverent worship. And these congregations are finding historic Reformed worship more conducive to the service of God, to the cultivation of Christian disciple-ship, and even more culturally adaptable than the approaches of the fad-chasing churches around them (and those churches are everywhere, having been exported by North Americans).

Reverent

Reformed worship is reverent. If worship is meeting with God, how could it be otherwise? It is precisely the reverence and awe of the greatness of God that characterizes Reformed worship at its best. All of the ministers and congregations mentioned above would agree with Old: "The greatest single contribution which the Reformed liturgical heritage can make to contemporary . . . Protestantism is its sense of the majesty and sovereignty of God, its sense of reverence, of simple dignity, its conviction that worship must above all serve the praise of God."[21]

This then is our corporate worship manifesto, our call for the doxological reformation of the church: *sola scriptura* and *soli deo gloria*.

---

21. Old, *Worship*, 176-77.

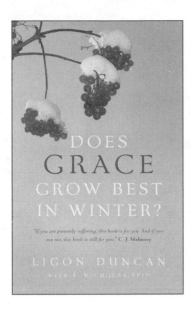

"Why is this happening to me? How can I get through this? *Can* I get through this?"

Learning some of the purposes for suffering, how it connects us with our Lord and his people, and what God's Word says to us in the midst of our pain enables us to glorify him in the most troubling times.

With a wealth of Scripture, a focus on the passion and sympathy of Jesus, and thoughtful questions for reflection or group discussion, this book will help to transform not only your outlook on suffering, but your life.

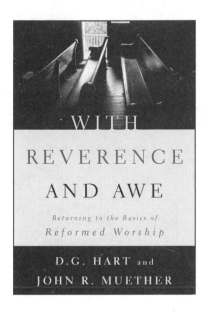

Even among Reformed Christians, *worship* is a fighting word. Conflicting expectations for worship reveal that there is significant confusion about its nature, purpose, and practice.

Originally designed for Sunday school classes, this book is a primer to the fundamentals of worship, drawing from Scripture and Reformed confessions. By overviewing how Reformed theology informs the way we think about, put together, and participate in a worship service, Hart and Muether prepare us to gather corporately for worship in ways that are appropriate to our Triune God.

Have you experienced worship services that downplayed their focus on God's presence to emphasize fellowship and ministry? Or ones whose "worship" had little sense of believers' coming together to minister to one another? How do we regain the right balance in our services?

David Peterson will teach you the biblical foundations of worship, the meaning and purpose of gathering together, and patterns and varieties of service models. Discover how to structure each service to take worshipers on a meaningful journey together.

"Biblical, practical, and insightful."
—**Bob Kauflin**, Director, Sovereign Grace Music

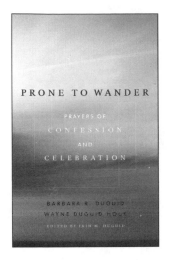
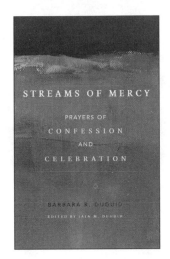

Confessing our sins might seem like a gloomy business . . . but exposing the specifics of our struggles with sin leads to celebration! It points us back to the good news of the gospel, our great Savior, and our forgiveness through God's grace.

Inspired by the Puritan classic *The Valley of Vision*, the prayers in these two volumes are ideal for use in church services or personal devotions. They open with a scriptural call of confession, confess specific sins, thank the Father for Jesus' perfect life and death in our place, ask for the help of the Spirit in pursuing holiness, and close with an assurance of pardon.

"[*Prone to Wander*] has many virtues. . . . The book covers the whole of the Christian life. I love its overall aims and method."
—Leland Ryken